Transformation:

Creating a Heart Renewed to **God**

Why do we choose Gossip?
Daily Inspiration and Journal

Dr. Mavis E. Morisseau

 Sula Too
Publishing

The Scriptures were denoted from various versions
of the Bible.

Editing:
Evangelist Phyllis Jordan
Karleta Chester Minister
Frank Jones

Layout and Illustrator: Tonya Mills

ISBN: 979-8-9865280-6-9 (Paperback Edition)
Printed and bound in the United States of America
February 2023

Published by Sula Too Publishing Tampa, Florida
For information about this title or to order books and/or
electronic media, contact the publisher: Sula Too Publishing
www.sulatoo.com/publishing 813-200-8878

How Elegant is the Blue Lotus

The blue Lotus symbolizes strength, tranquility, intelligence, and spiritual embodiment. The blue Lotus can be related to Mary in the bible because she was regarded as the queen of paradise.

In ancient Egypt the blue lotus represents rebirth. This meaning was inspired by the nature of the lotus's petals, which spread above water upon sensing sunlight and close during the night so the flower falls back under water. The lotus is mentioned in the book of Job 40:21-22 "Under the lotus plants he lies, in the shelter of the reeds and in the marsh. For his shade the lotus trees cover him; the willows of the brook surround him."

The lotus is not only beautiful in nature, but when worn in the hair or on the body its radiates and shows absolute peace and beauty.

Table of Contents

Dedication
Introduction
Foreword
Preface

Devotion Scriptures
Fortifications for the Mind, Heart, and Spirit

Dedication

This book is dedicated to my beautiful family: Dr. Mateen Diop, Ladii Rollins, Sariyah, Iyima Rollins, TaYon, Cheyenne, De'Jeh, Chavon, Devon Harris, Jonae, Chris, Micah, and Miela Scott, Ashonta, Alana, Amina, Audrey, Andre Johnson, Joseph, Nyjah, Paityn, Lailah Rollins, Mylan Morisseau, Samenta Morisseau and Zion, Dr. Kai Dupe, Jocelyn and Marvin Porter, Elsie Cyrs, Colby Cyrs, Darlene Wynn, Tracey Mitchell, whose love, support, and truth made this book possible.

To the True Worship Prophetic Kingdom Ministry Prayer Line family: Karleta Chester, Sydney Moreta, Sheridan Moreta, Min. Frank Jones, Deaconess Shirley Dower, Charlotte Knight, Keith Key, Dr. Rosalee Banks, Deaconess Bernadine Kimball, Pastor Sylvester Rawlings, Elder Kingwood, Prophetess Diana Pryme, Pastor Andra Standberry, Rev. Sandy Smith, Rev. Sharon Wallace, Pastor Kevin & Gaile Howell, Evangelist Phyllis Jordan, Evangelist Carolie and Tor Lenoir, Khiry Lenoir, Pastor Maurice Taylor, Deacon Nathaniel Rollins, Deacon Howard Rollins, Deacon Lester Pelamon, Deacon Oscar Osborn, Mother Samella Rounds, Elder Byron Rounds, Brother Sidney Mackey, Min. Janice and James Suitte, Rev. Dr Russell Groves, Pastor Rudolf McCoy, Rev. Matthew McCoy, Pastor W. Favorite, Rev. Maurice Taylor, Min. Brittney Monique Allen, Prophetess Nicole Payne, Overseer Yolanda Osborne Kohn, Min. Karyle and James Thornton, Min. Talia Bush, Pastor Kavin & Comet Bobbitt, Pastor Frank & Deidra Givens, Rev. Ernest & Catina Bridges, Mother Elizabeth Bridges, Elder Edward & Debra Smith, Evangelist Frankie & Felicia Branch, Elder Jonathan Powell, and the women at The Well.

Thank you for the love and encouragement.

Foreword I

I look at this woman's picture and she reflects a woman asking and being answered by God; a Woman seeking and finding God; a Woman Ushered through Open doors by God. A woman walking in her own Uniqueness of God's Anointing; strong - yet humbled, brought low – yet soaring to heights that allow God's Love to flow through her deepest depths.

And let me say this: God Has Shown Himself to be The Author and Finisher of this woman's life, Pastor Mavis Yvette Potter. God Did it for His daughter; He Spoke, and we all Saw What He Said! The child would look in her eyes, and she would hear God's Direction. That's what I saw, even as it was being said.

She came to us with her pain, my heart immediately reached to the Heavens; Father what do I say to her, and He Said, "Be you". Where's that in the Bible, I thought? I NEVER heard The Father Say that to me before. "Rest in me, do not allow your heart to become troubled, quiet your spirit, and believe Me". That became my silent prayer request. "This Is The Day, a Beautiful Day that I Have Made, and you all came before Me rejoicing and stood firm to be glad in it; you were all on one accord too; why would I not give you all your hearts' desire - I counted the hearts", He Said (my mouth fell open). And He said it in past tense, like He showed me to prayer.

She was hurt, not yet realizing God Had Already Worked a Miracle; but not so hurt that The Joy of The Lord could not find her spirit – she Allowed Him, and received her Strength; and then, I heard it in her voice "Come on somebody, who else wants to love on The Lord?" after we all sang with her, and prayed for her, and stretched for her – it was Amazing how she came back on to the line and handled her ministry. That's The Father I know when I'm hurting, the time of pain is shortened through the Indwelling and a Receiving of The Loving Truth for the matter. In her weakness, she submitted to The Father, resisted the thoughts of the enemy (hearing The Word of God), and renewed her mind to trust "How" His Molding would make her Strong – and...

Suddenly - she experiences the Presence of The Father Calling the devil a liar right before her eyes; and He Performed Miracles in direct opposition to what the enemy had designed - and Revealed the Perfect Plan that was in action for her, all along. He Made Good on His Promise that that Good Thing Would not be withheld from her; the Lovely thing, the Pure thing, the True thing, the thing of Good Report - and she held her newborn grand-daughter in her arms, still fresh from her now grave-clothes, in a way that presented her untouched by anyone until "Grandmother" welcomed her to the world; and she reached down and Blessed her with a kiss with His Spirit. I have heard and seen God Show up in her life; she invites Him to change her, and He's taking her with Him from glory to glory.

Pictures of her and her beautiful 2yr old grand-daughter, then pictures of holding her newborn grand-daughter – He Had Done It – Miracles - The Spirit of Joy hovered over me all day long. I was so happy to see God Answering our interceding fervent prayers of agreement, and Working Miracle after Miracle after Miracle, Loving on her; I mean, you couldn't help but wonder, am I the only one seeing this? Purpose.

Sonia Diana Pryme

Foreword II

Greetings in the name of our Lord and Savior Jesus Christ,

It is truly an honor Pastor Mavis Evette Morisseau, to write the Forward for your new book "Transformation: Creating a Heart Renewed to God" Glory to God for these words that He has placed in my heart through the Holy Spirit…!

What a blessing it is having you in my life and seeing yet another major piece of your work come to fruition. God's favor is truly upon you, and you are such an inspiration to me. Each day I bear witness, through you, as to what He can and will do in the lives of those who believe in Him ("Won't He Do It?")

As God continues to shape and mold you into the woman that He has purposed you to be, I am inspired by the works of His mighty hand. I bear witness to His word being made manifest in you. Pastor Mavis Evette your life is a manifestation of His glory.

You bring glory and honor to our Lord and Savior Jesus Christ in all that you do. In all that you do God's love shines through. You are the epitome of the Virtuous Woman found in Proverbs 31:10-31.

As the Founder and Pastor of True Worship Prophetic Kingdom Ministries Prayer line, (Church With and Without Walls (formerly Bethel House of God Prayer line)), each day you touch the lives of believers all around the world.

As a Mother and Grandmother, "your teachings are a graceful wreath upon the heads of your children and an ornamental wreath adorning their necks" (Proverbs 1:8-9). "You continue to teach them diligently and talk of them when you sit in your house, when you walk by the way, when you lie down and when you rise up" {Deuteronomy 6:7). "Your children will rise up and call you blessed" (Proverbs 31:28). Praise the Lord!

As a Sister and Friend, your integrity, perseverance, and commitment to excellence is an inspiration to us all. Your commitment to academic excellence, attaining a Bachelor of Sciences, Master of Divinity, Master's in Creative Movement and/or Honorary Doctor of Divinity is a testament of His Goodness and Mercies towards us. His purpose for your life being fulfilled!

Congratulations my dear sister and friend, the Lord is blessing you in a mighty way and I celebrate you mighty woman of God as He continues to use you to be a blessing to us all.

Trust and Believe, as we touch and agree, the best (seller) is yet to come… Halleluiah!!!

Lovingly,
Minister, Mildred (Kisha) Polite Smith
Clifton Park, NY

Foreword III

And from the days of John the Baptist until now the kingdom of heaven suffereth violence, and the violent take it by force.

Matthew 11:12

The Kingdom of God is a battlefield, and we are at war. Just because we are in God's army doesn't mean that we have on our whole armor. Many of us have been on the front lines and have wounds to show it. Even though the battle is already won, some of us are still suffering. We have spiritual PTSD (post- traumatic stress disorder) because of the attacks of the enemy. Some soldiers lack proper combat training and can't take the intensity of the fight. They go AWOL (absent without leave). Others become POWs (prisoners of war) because they have been locked down in spiritual jail subject to enemy forces, and there seems like there is no escape route.

God has a solution for those who have been humiliated, degraded, brainwashed, sick, rejected, and dealing with psychological warfare. Battle scars can disrupt and impair our daily lives and our walk with God. These open wounds from war can be healed with God's Word. The Bible is our combat training manual that contains military strategies to subdue the enemy in our lives. But we have to apply the tactics.

God says in Isaiah 61:
"The Spirit of the Lord GOD is upon Me,
Because the LORD has anointed Me
To preach good tidings to the poor;
He has sent Me to heal the brokenhearted,
To proclaim liberty to the captives,
And the opening of the prison to those who are bound;

God is using Pastor Mavis Morisseau to fulfill this promise He made in Isaiah 61 in this book. "God never causes our trials and tribulations. The enemy (Satan) is the source of all evil, but God will use the enemy's attacks for our good". God wants to heal our war wounds. Through this organized study of the Word of God we will learn that there is perfect freedom and healing in God's service.

"Suffer hardship with me, as a good soldier of Christ Jesus." II Timothy 2:3

Minister Jeanette Jones

Foreword IV

Every once in a while, God will grace us with a person here on earth whose life has been ripped right from the pages of the Bible itself. And while each Christ follower is tasked to be a sequel to the Bible, part of the great commission, we meet a Mavis Evette who has gone far and beyond the call of duty.

Nowhere have I had firsthand knowledge of anyone to grow, develop, and transform not only in their educational endeavors but also in their spiritual journey in just five short years. Nowhere.

From the time I first met Dr. Mavis, I knew something was extraordinarily different about her. She has since accelerated from Minister Mavis to Pastor Mavis to now Dr. Mavis. But the irony of it all is that God has always seen her as Dr. Mavis. That's right.

Mavis Evette was Dr. Mavis even when she was being abused, misused, overlooked even misunderstood. And here's why. God gifted this woman with LOVE. Dr. Mavis will love anyone right where they are even as a child, adolescent, and young woman. Yes, even in her MESS. That's when you know where a person is really gifted is in their mess. Our mess does become our messages if we share it with others.

That's what this devotional book is about. Dr. Mavis is sharing with others how God has transformed her messes into messages of daily doses of spiritual inspiration for any situation. Such as a daily dose of love, forgiveness, and hope and prayer just to name a few. All geared toward helping the reader ultimately trust more in God, Yeshua, Jesus.

Dr. Mavis is fulfilling her recognized call as God continues to anoint her to preach the Good News to those who hide in fear, to declare freedom for those in captivity, to spread love (the necessary ointment to heal the broken-hearted), to exchange beauty for ashes, give oil of joy for those who mourn, and provide a garment of praise for the spirit of heaviness.

This devotional book is a love tool that shares Dr. Mavis' daily healing message of hope (part of her legacy). Whatever situation you find yourself in, I'm certain, there's a message in this devotional book that will speak LOVE into your atmosphere.

I know without a shadow of doubt in Dr. Mavis' words … "Fall in love with Jesus and I promise you He will love you back. Hallelujah!"

I love you my dear Friend. Congratulations on yet another outstanding accomplishment, receiving your doctoral degree, and another literary work. To God be the glory for what He's doing in your life!

Andra Allen Standberry
Founder, Pastor & Author
Word of Life Fellowship Ministries, Inc. Austin, Texas

Foreword V

Getting to know the author of this cherished work from the hands of my friend, my sister in Christ, Dr. Mavis Evette Morisseau, has been an honor and a pleasure.

I give GOD all the glory and honor for making me worthy of such a friend. A friend, who I have known for a brief 4 years of ministry. Our conversations, our friendship, and love for one another is far-reaching and everlasting. You can't buy eternal friendship for eternal love only comes from the Father.

My life journey has been filled with many trials and tribulations. But because True Worship Prophetic Kingdom Ministry and its members have taken the time to love, encourage, and pray for me and my family, I have endured, persevered, and overcame many challenges. I appreciate my True Worship Prophetic Kingdom Ministry family. A ministry without walls that has reached international audiences from the United States to the shores of Africa.

The birthing of this ministry through Dr. Mavis E. Morisseau has been my lifeline to staying in GOD's grace and under the shadow of the Almighty. As we worship together, we bond in the spirit, we break bread together and are strengthened. Each time we reach for the Father, He reaches for us. Each time we call on the Name of Jesus, He is there. Never out of reach, have we felt God's hand on our lives.

Dr. Mavis and I share a special bond because our testimonies of sexual abuse and domestic violence are very similar. However, we are no longer victims, but GOD's phenomenal survivors. Each of our lives are the personification of GODs miraculous power and perfect peace.

My friend's intellect and courage is demonstrated time and time again as she overcomes daily challenges that arise. Dr. Mavis is constantly, criticized by a world that does not love GOD's children and hated by the enemy because of the anointing on her life, a beautiful Prophetic Ministry, and her knowledge of GOD's Word.

Dr. Mavis Morisseau freely sows her spirit into the lives of so many others. As she sows God's love, I ask that the Lord God Almighty fill her cup with an overflow of Joy, Peace, Love, Goodness, and Kindness. I thank the Lord for allowing me to see the manifestation of healing and growth through His Word and her journey. Our connection in the spirit is forever joined; together we are GOD's workmanship, and we give HIM GLORY!!!

Forever God's
Workmanship, Evangelist Phyllis
Lizzie Etta Jordan
Retired U.S. Army

Preface

Amazing Grace, how sweet the sound that saved a wretch like me. I once was lost, but now I'm found, was blind but now I see.

Luke 8:10 And He said, "The knowledge of the secrets of the kingdom of God has been given to you, but to others I speak in parables, so that, "'though seeing, they may not see; though hearing, they may not understand.

God already knew that Dr. Mavis would see the light for He alone created the tapestry of her being. People along her journey may have counted her out, but the saying goes, "If God takes you to it, He will bring you through it." She is undeniably a warrior, survivor, and a champion in the Kingdom of God.

It has been a divine experience witnessing the seasons of transformation through the shedding, healing, rebuilding, and restoring. The road was not easy but, Dr. Mavis met the challenges of life head on with prayer and a steadfast commitment to God.

Dr. Mavis' level of growth from Anointed Vessels to Bethel House of God to True Worship Prophetic Kingdom Ministry is a testament of her strength, spiritual discipline, maturity in Yeshua, and God's manifested Chayil Glory. Her life in Yeshua is not just focused on herself, but inclusive of her family, community, and an expanse of cultures all around the world.

Dr. Mavis prays with anyone, anywhere, and at any time boldly proclaiming the Gospel. I love that God has placed her in a position of which she continuously changes lives. She has opened her home to many over the years as a haven for spiritual encouragement, love, peace, and guidance.

God continues to do great things through Dr. Mavis. This book has come to fruition because she has conquered defeat at many levels resulting in a change of heart, mind, and direction. Elohim has allowed her to see with brand new eyes, live in "Big Faith", and have a heart for those in need as she purposes to be better than yesterday every day and promise to live Yeshua on the inside.

I thank God for being close enough to see His works, His Glory through you.

Reverend Stephanie Harley
True Worship Prophetic Kingdom   Ministry

Introduction

We are compelled to be continually watchful--to keep the lid on the poison, to keep the discipline of our speech in place, because we know the power to destroy with our tongues is present as often as we speak.

Spread gossip, and people will not trust you. Speak with sarcasm and insults, and people will not follow you. Yet what is especially on James' mind is not the reaction of others to your speech but the spreading of sin from your speech to the rest of your life. Being hateful with your tongue, and you will be hateful with other aspects of your behavior. If you do not discipline and purify your speech, you will not discipline or purify the rest of your life.

With the tongue we praise our Lord and Father, and with it we curse human beings, who have been made in God's likeness. Out of the same mouth come praise and cursing. My brothers and sisters, this should not be. Can both fresh water and saltwater flow from the same spring? My brothers and sisters, can a fig tree bear olives, or a grapevine bear figs? Neither can a salt spring produce fresh water. (James 5:9-12)

I say then walk in the Spirit, and you shall not fulfill the lust of the flesh. For the flesh lust against the Spirit, and the Spirit against the flesh; and these are contrary to one another, so that you do not do the things that you wish. (Galatians 5:16-17)

Let the word of Christ dwell in you richly in all wisdom, teaching, and admonishing one another in psalms, hymns, and spiritual songs, singing with grace in your hearts to the Lord. (Colossians 3:16.)

My sheep hear my voice, I know them, and they follow me. (John 10:27)

Blessed is the man who listens to me, watching daily at my gates. Waiting in the post of my doors. (Proverbs 8:34)

Inspiration

The Bible is the inspired Word of God. When we read it and study it, we find our way to God, we find our way to His will for us, and we find how we can conform ourselves to His will.

Foundational Principles
The Lord's Prayer

9   "This, then, is how you should pray:
    "'Our Father in heaven,
    hallowed be your name,
10 your kingdom come,
    your will be done,
    on earth as it is in heaven.
11 Give us today our daily bread.
12 And forgive us our debts,
    as we also have forgiven our debtors.
13 And lead us not into temptation,
    but deliver us from the evil one."

    For yours is the kingdom and the power
    and the glory forever. Amen.

תַּעֲרֹךְ לְפָנַי שֻׁלְחָן נֶגֶד צֹרְרָי

my enemies   in front of   a table   before me   You prepare

דִּשַּׁנְתָּ בַשֶּׁמֶן רֹאשִׁי כּוֹסִי רְוָיָה

overflows   my cup   my head   with oil   You anoint

Psalm 23

The LORD is my shepherd;
I shall not want.

2   He makes me to lie down in green pastures;
     He leads me beside the still waters.
3   He restores my soul;
     He leads me in the paths of righteousness
     For His name's sake.
4   Yea, though I walk through the valley of the shadow of death,
     I will fear no evil;
     For You are with me;
     Your rod and Your staff, they comfort me.
5   You prepare a table before me in the presence of my enemies;
     You anoint my head with oil;
     My cup runs over.
6   Surely goodness and mercy shall follow me
     All the days of my life;
     And I will dwell in the house of the LORD
     Forever.

Matthew 5:3-11

The Beatitudes

And seeing the multitudes, He went up on a mountain, and when He was seated His disciples came to Him.

2   Then He opened His mouth and taught them, saying:

3   "Blessed are the poor in spirit,
For theirs is the kingdom of heaven.

4   Blessed are those who mourn,
For they shall be comforted.

5   Blessed are the meek,
For they shall inherit the earth.

6   Blessed are those who hunger and thirst for righteousness,
For they shall be filled.

7   Blessed are the merciful,
For they shall obtain mercy.

8   Blessed are the pure in heart,
For they shall see God.

9   Blessed are the peacemakers,
For they shall be called sons of God.

10   Blessed are those who are persecuted for righteousness' sake,
For theirs is the kingdom of heaven.

11   "Blessed are you when they revile and persecute you and say all kinds of evil against you falsely for My sake.

12   Rejoice and be exceedingly glad, for great is your reward in heaven, for so they persecuted the prophets who were before you.

Exodus 20:1-17

The Ten Commandments

And God spoke all these words, saying:

2   "I am the LORD your God, who brought you out of the land of Egypt, out of the house of bondage.

3   "You shall have no other gods before Me.

4   "You shall not make for yourself a carved image—any likeness of anything that is in heaven above, or that is in the earth beneath, or that is in the water under the earth; 5 you shall not bow down to them nor serve them. For I, the LORD your God, am a jealous God, visiting the iniquity of the fathers upon the children to the third and fourth generations of those who hate Me, 6 but showing mercy to thousands, to those who love Me and keep My commandments.

7   "You shall not take the name of the LORD your God in vain, for the LORD will not hold him guiltless who takes His name in vain.

8   "Remember the Sabbath day, to keep it holy. 9 Six days you shall labor and do all your work, 10 but the seventh day is the Sabbath of the LORD your God. In it you shall do no work: you, nor your son, nor your daughter, nor your male servant, nor your female servant, nor your cattle, nor your stranger who is within your gates. 11 For in six days the LORD made the heavens and the earth, the sea, and all that is in them, and rested the seventh day. Therefore, the LORD blessed the Sabbath day and hallowed it.

12   "Honor your father and your mother, that your days may be long upon the land which the LORD your God is giving you. 13 "You shall not murder. 14 "You shall not commit adultery. 15 "You shall not steal. 16 "You shall not bear false witness against your neighbor. 17 "You shall not covet your neighbor's house; you shall not covet your neighbor's wife, nor his male servant, nor his female servant, nor his ox, nor his donkey, nor anything that is your neighbor's."

Chapter 1
Recognize the Sin

The words of a gossip are like choice morsels they go down to a man's inward parts. (Proverbs 18:8, 26:22)

The first rule of war is to know your enemy.

Before we can resist gossip, we must recognize it. That's not as easy to do as it may sound. It is not always easy to recognize the moment when our "small talk" becomes sinful talk. In fact, if you're like me, then you regularly ask yourself during conversations, "Should I be saying this?" or, "Should I be listening to this?"

You may even find yourself questioning what makes gossip wrong. Is it when it is said? Who says it? To whom it is told? We often give ourselves small passes. Gossip is okay if were just chatting with our husband or sister, right? What is gossip anyway? Is it always malicious? The line becomes increasingly distorted, and confusion sets in about the definition of gossip. Deciding what is or isn't gossip is certainly a challenge.

The hardest part about recognizing gossip is that it does not come with a warning label. Wouldn't it be great if a sign like this would flash above the heads of the people with whom we're talking?

Nevertheless, this is not what happens. No, normally, there we are, just talking with someone, and seemingly out of nowhere this juicy piece of news about someone else presents itself and asks us to swallow it. The Bible says, *"The words of gossip are like choice morsels; they go down to a man's most inward parts" (Proverb 18:8, 26:22)*

Choice Morsels

"Choice Morsels" are tasty things that we want to devour quickly. They are the best, most attractive things to eat. They are like a bowl of potato chips left on the kitchen counter.

What happens in most families if mom puts a plate of cookies out on the kitchen counter in the late afternoon? I don't know about your family, but at our place, those things are gone like the wind!

But let's say there are cookies on the counter. What happens if you eat the whole bag before dinner yourself? You're probably going to feel sick. Gossip is like that. It goes "down to a man's most inward parts." Gossip takes great going down, but it has lasting and poisonous effects on our hearts.

But again, what is sinful gossip? I'm glad you asked. Here is a one-sentence summary of the Bible's teaching on gossip: Sinful gossip is bearing bad news behind someone else's back and out of a bad heart. This definition has three parts.

Definition Part 1: Bearing Bad News

Gossip is, obviously, a "talking" thing. As we saw, our opening scripture says, "The words of a gossip are like choice morsels." Gossip is sharing, communicating, and transmitting stories. These stories flow in both directions: talking and listening.

First, talking. Proverbs says, *"A gossip betrays a confidence, so avoid a man who talks too much" (20:19)*. The old King James word for a gossip in Proverbs 20:19 is a "talebearer" or one who carries a story. Gossiping is often sharing someone else's secret. Have you ever done that? Have you ever had it done to you? It feels awful to find out that someone gave away your secret. It is a betrayal by talking.

Then there is listening. Proverbs also says, *"Wrongdoers eagerly listen to gossip: liars pay close attention to slander" (17:4)*. Sometimes even just receiving that spicy piece of gossip without stopping the conversation (or at least saying something) is sinful- almost as sinful as speaking it.

Gossip on Social Media

Of course, the bearing of bad news is not done just by talking in person. Technology has made it possible for us to gossip long distance. We can gossip on the phone. We can gossip online. We can tweet our gossip on twitter!

Anything that can be used for great good can also be used for evil, especially if it involves a lot of words. The Bible teaches this: *"When words are many, sin is not absent, but he who holds his tongue is wise" (Proverbs 10:19)*.

So, sin gossip for me, might be pushing the "Send" button on my phone, or the "Publish" button on my blog or the "Share" button on my Facebook account. Remember, whatever is said online is pretty much permanent. Think first.

Three Types of Bad News

The content of sinful gossip is never neutral. It is always "bad news" of at least one of three kinds.

Bad Information. Sharing bad information, lies about someone behind their back is sinful gossip. Worse, if you know the story is false, then it is not just gossip, it is also slander! Have you ever had your reputation hurt by bad information that someone had spread about you?

The Lord promises us that *"a false witness will not go unpunished, and he who pours out lies will not go free" (Proverb 19:5)*.

Of course, the bad information might be something that you think is true but really is not.

Bad news about someone. On the other hand, the story being shared might actually be true and only about something bad that someone had done. This is what I call shameful truth. Some of us has been taught that if something is true, then it's not gossip. Not so. Gossip is also foolishly spreading that awful truth about someone. Proverbs tells us that *"a gossip betrays a confidence, but a trustworthy man keeps a secret (11:13)*. The secrets revealed by gossip are often the skeletons in someone's closet that do not really need to get out.

A biblical phrase for this is *"a bad report" (Hebrew dibbah)*. A bad report is what Joseph brought to Jacob about his brothers in (Genesis 37:2). We don't know exactly what the young men were up to but given what we do know about Joseph's ten brothers, it was probably something they shouldn't have been doing. So, Joseph probably was not lying, but he was, at the very least, being an annoying tattletale. Tattling is gossiping to someone in authority instead of someone uninvolved. Proverbs says, *"Whoever spreads slander is a fool" (Proverbs 10:18)*. For example, let's say one of your friends recently did something bad, and you heard about it. He cut someone off in traffic. She lied to her spouse. He cheated a coworker. She hit her mother. Whatever. Your friend actually did some shameful thing.

Catch this: you don't have to talk about any of it with your other friends!

I know it's hard to refrain. As our key Scripture passage says, "The words of a gossip are like choice morsels." They are incredibly difficult to resist.

By the way, you may have to memorize Proverbs 18:8 and 26:22 in the King James Version, and right now you may be scratching your head and saying, "Hey wait a minute! That verse says, 'The words of a talebearer are as wounds!' There is a big difference between wounds and choice morsels!"

The difference between the two versions is that translators of the King James Bible thought that the Hebrew root being used here was one that means to hammer or strike something (halam). And that rings true, doesn't it? The words of a gossip are harmful. They are a kick in the gut.

But most scholars today believe that there is a different Hebrew root underlying this word: laham. This root word depicts savory or delicious morsels that you can hardly resist and want to swallow right down.

Back in Solomon's day a choice morsel wasn't made of chocolate and strawberries. It may have been various nuts and raisins, or figs mixed with honey for something sweet to eat. Or, even more likely, it was a choice piece of meat.

Bad news, shameful news is like that too for you and me. Bad news is attractive but not good for us. There is something wrong within us that makes us want to know and to talk about the shameful things that other people do.

Bad news for someone. A third kind of bad news is neither false nor true but is a projection of something bad happening to someone. In Psalm 41 King David got really sick, and his enemies rejoiced and started to gossip about him. David wrote,

My enemies say of me in malice. "When will he die, and his name perish?" Whenever one comes to see me, he speaks falsely, while his heart gathers slander; then he goes out and spreads it abroad. All my enemies whisper together against me; they imagine the worst for me, saying, *"A vile disease has beset him; he will never get up from the place where he lives." (41:5-8)*

That is gossip too. David had not done anything shameful, but his enemies were two faced. They came in saying, "Oh, poor you," and then went out to spread the bad news that he was going to die.

Have you ever had this happen to you? People say, "He's going to lose his job" or, "He's not going to make the team." They project, "She's going to get kicked out of school" or, "Her husband is going to leave her." They whisper. "They're going to lose their house." Gossip is bad news wickedly projected for someone else.

Definition Part 2: Speaking Behind Someone's Back

By anyone's definition gossip happens when the person you are talking about is not there. Some translations of Proverbs 18:8 and 26:22 use the word "whisperer" instead of "gossip" or "talebearer." A whisperer is someone who talks about you behind your back. Therefore, gossip is clandestine-and intentionally so!

You see, it is so much easier (and more interesting) to talk about someone when they are not around.

Before you talk (or before you continue to talk) about someone who is not present, ask yourself the following:

- Would I say this if he were here?
- Would I receive this bad news about her in the same way if she were present?
- Am I hiding this conversation from someone?
- Would I want someone else to talk this way about me if I were out of the room?

Yeah, But What about…?

Let me clear up a possible misunderstanding. The Bible is not teaching that we should never talk about people who are not present. We certainly can say good things about people who are not with us. In fact, we should absolutely turn gossip around and spread good news about people!

Also, there are times when we must talk about people who are not present and even share bad things about them. Parents, teachers, elders, and pastors, even friends, teammates, coworkers, and neighbors all have to do that sometimes. This falls in line with the biblical principle of warning others.

Sometimes we need to seek counsel from a wise person about our conflicts and problems. Seeking counsel may involve sharing the shameful things that someone else has done without that person being there. It is certainly not sinful gossip to truly seek out help. On the other hand, we can also mask our desire to gossip by claiming that we are just seeking counsel. The key to sharing circumstances with people in a right way is to keep loving others even when we must talk about them and even if they are our enemies. Simply put, we just need to apply Jesus' Golden Rule to any difficult situation. If you must talk about someone when they are not present, make sure that you are treating them as you would want to be treated.

Definition Part 3: Unclean Heart

Gossip comes out of a bad heart. That is, gossip is caused by something that is wrong at the core of our beings. We are attracted to the "choice morsels" of gossip because of something already wrong in our "inmost parts." Accepting this is the most important key in resisting gossip.

The Lord Jesus taught that *"out of the overflow of the heart the mouth speaks" (Matthew12:34)*. The heart is the control center of a person. It is the inner you, the real you. The Bible also teaches that we live from the heart. Proverbs says, *"Above all else, guard your heart, for it is the wellspring of life (4:23)*. Our motives spring from our hearts. Our sinful motivations for speaking about or listening to any form of bad news makes gossip sinful. Therefore, in recognizing gossip the most important question for us to answer is "Why?"

- Why am I this?
- Why am I listening to this?
- Why am I attracted to this bad news?

It could be because of jealousy or anger or hate. Or it could be the result of boredom, pride, or the fear of people. There are a number of sinful hearts motivations that can produce sinful gossip. The good news is that the gospel of Jesus Christ has answers for them all.

Learning How to Resist

Proverbs 18:8 and 26:22 offer only a warning. *"Beware of gossip"*. They do not tell us how to resist those choice morsels---just that we need to. But now that we have a biblically informed definition to use when we attempt to recognize gossip, we can begin to think more clearly about gospel strategies for resisting gossip. Some of those strategies include:

- Bearing good news
- Being up front, and loving those we talk about and talk to
- Having a changed heart that loves God and loves people

I was a big fan of Charm: The Next Generation. The greatest enemy was the spirit of Fear during that season of Charm series was a demon called

Barbus. He always came to kill, steal, and destroy humanity. Basically, the enemy was part of one great big hole that swallowed up people into its world. There was no individualism in Charm, just "the collective." When the demons came to town their favorite phrase was, "Kill them all who believe in the greater good!

I know that we must not conform to the world's pattern, people lie out of fear, shame, guilt, and gossip to fit in, so what you watch on T.V. also makes a difference, even the music you feed into your spirit can be bad news.

Jesus Christ died to set us free from sin. *"He himself bore our sins in his body on the tree, so that we might die to sins and live for righteousness" (1 Peter 2:24).* Resistance is not futile. Doesn't the Bible insist that we are to *"resist the devil, and he will flee" (James4:7)*? The Lord Jesus empowers us to die to sins and live for righteousness. One of the chief ways He does that is through promises like the ones we find in First Corinthians 10:13.

A Great and Precious Promise: A Way of Escape

The apostle Paul told the Corinthians, *"No temptation has seized you except what is common to man" (1 Cor. 10:13).* The urge to gossip is not extraordinary. We should not feel as if we are the first to ever experience it. I'm sure that the Lord Jesus was tempted to gossip (although, Praise God, he never gave in (Hebrews 4:15).

But Paul went on to say, *"And God is faithful; He will not let you be tempted beyond what you can bear" (1 Cor. 10:13).* We have to believe what Paul said, even though it will seldom feel as if it is true.

Paul finished the verse with the promise, *"But when you are tempted, (God) will also provide a way out so that you can stand up under it" (10:13).* What a great and precious promise! Our job is to trust God's promise and to look for the "way out" which will always be available. The temptation may not go away. We may even have to continue to "stand up under it." Yet although it is not easy, it is possible to win against sinful gossip.

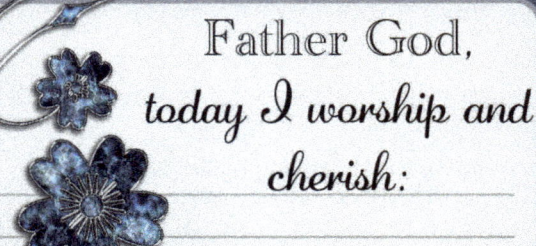

Date:

Father God, today I worship and cherish:

What are the prayer request that I should ask GOD for today?

What is GOD calling me to do today?

Chapter 2
Why Do We Choose Sin?

Even if some people don't like to read, everyone loves a story. We delight in hearing someone share a tale, whether it is funny, sad, strange, or happy. And many of us love to tell stories ourselves.

The Historical Story

Stories are an integral part of our lives. They are how we figure out our world and our place in it. The Bible is full of stories. Most of the Old Testament and all the Gospels and Acts are narratives. The other parts of Scriptures, such as the Psalms, Proverbs, and the letters, include loads of storytelling features. All these biblical stories are like tributaries that are carried along and then joined together to form one great river—the grand story of redemption.

One summary of this great story says, *"For God so loved the world that He gave His one and only Son, that whoever believes in him shall not perish but have eternal life" (John 3:16)*. Eternal life and eternal death are bound up in our believing or not believing. In the story of Jesus. The simple version for this story is "the gospel." The gospel is good news-the best story-and it is powerful. As the apostle Paul says, *"I am not ashamed of the gospel, because it is the power of God for the salvation of everyone who believes" (Romans 1:16)*.

So, it's no wonder that we love stories! We are living in one.

Stories Gone Bad

The problem is not that we love stories but that we can love stories too much, and especially, we can love the wrong stories. We saw in the previous chapter that sinful gossip tells a bad story. It is bad news. And while there are times when sharing bad news is necessary (especially when it leads up to good news), bearing bad news can be antithetical to the gospel itself.

In Genesis 3, we read that the serpent in the garden told the woman a bad story about God. He questioned her, *"Did God really say...?" (3:1)*. The serpent slandered God's reputation, and when his bad story was believed, the effect was devastating on all human history. Every small bit of sinful gossip in daily life is an evil echo of what went wrong at the very beginning. In fact, gossip is the same ugly sin played out again and again. Gossip is believing the ancient lie that we can attempt to play God by destroying others with the power of our words. Gossip is not just breaking a rule, it is perversely living out Satan's lies, which we would rather believe than the truth.

And therefore, sadly, we are attracted to the wrong stories. Bad news travels fast because it is popular. A few years ago, a prominent Christian working in government was found to have been involved in a petty theft. I don't know why, but I became addicted to his story. I kept searching the Internet for more details and reading every discussion about the situation that I could find on any blog. There was no good reason for me to inform myself about it, but I could hardly stop myself from digging for more. This is a perfect example of how our hearts are spring-loaded to love bad stories.

Overflow

In Matthew 12, we read that Jesus denounced the Pharisees for accusing Him of being in league with Satan. Their accusations were bad words, if I have ever heard any! Our Lord Jesus said,

Make a tree good and its fruit will be good or make a tree bad and its fruit will be bad, for a tree is recognized by its fruit. You brood of vipers, how can you who are evil say anything good? For out of the overflow of the heart the mouth speaks. The good man brings good things out of the good stored up in him, and the evil man brings evil things out of the evil stored up in him. But I tell you that men will have to give account on the day of judgment for every careless word they have spoken. For by your words, you will be acquitted, and by your words you will be condemned. (12:33-37)

Let's call this the principle of overflow. We gossip (or say anything bad) because bad words overflow from out of bad hearts.

Jesus compared people to trees. If the heart of the tree-the root system and trunk— is healthy, then the fruit of the tree will be good too. But if the root system is diseased, then the fruit will be worthless. We can tell what's in someone's heart by what comes out in the fruit. The same is true with us. Our words reveal what is in our hearts.

The Lord Jesus was saying to the Pharisees, being snakelike (living out the bad story from the Garden of Eden), could not say anything good. It was not in their nature. It was not in their heart. As Jesus said to them, *"The good man brings good things out of the good stored up in him, and the evil man brings evil things out of the evil stored up in him" (Matthew 12:35).*

Everything that comes out of our mouths reflects something that is deep within.

That's what Jesus was saying. Good small talk, good stories, come from good that is "stored up" in the heart. Sinful gossip comes out of the evil that is "stored up" in the human heart.

This is true even for believers in Jesus who now have new hearts from God (Ezekiel 36:26). The residue of indwelling sin lingers within us and continues to create evil motivations even when we are Christ followers.

Sometimes we cannot correctly discern our own motives. Our hearts can be very deceptive, even with ourselves. But God knows. The Bible teaches, *"All a man's ways seem innocent to him, but motives are weighed by the Lord"*

(Proverbs 16:2). It also says that *"Death and Destruction lie open before the Lord---how much more the hearts of men!" (Proverbs15:11)*. God knows and understands what is going on inside of us, even when we do not.

Matthew 12 is not the only place in which we see Jesus teaching the principle of overflow. We read in Matthew 15 that Jesus also says, "Out of the heart comes evil thoughts, murder, adultery, sexual immorality, theft, false testimony, slander" (15:19). It is not just our sinful words that proceed from the heart but all our sins--- including listening to sinful gossip.

In Matthew 12 passage, He said, *"I tell you that men will have to give account on the day of judgment for every careless word they have spoken. For by your words, you will be acquitted, and by your words you will be condemned" (12:36-37).*

That is sobering. Just think about giving an account, not just for every malicious word that you and I have spoken, but for every careless, sinless, idle word! Words are serious. They do not just hit the air and then drift away. They are remembered. God is listening, and we will have to answer to Him.

There Is Hope

God is in the business of changing our hearts. Believers do still have indwelling sin, but our sin is not greater than our Savior! Our indwelling sin is much like Saddam Hussein hiding away in a death dark hole, thinking that he can still regain power by trying to coordinate the wreaking of havoc on the new regime. Though still dangerous, sin is a defeated enemy. I like to say, "Sin is still resident, but it is not president!" The Bible says that we have been *"set free from sin and have become slaves to God (Romans 6:22)*. The Lord is our new master, and He is really good.

Looking Ahead

So where do we go from here? How do we break away from the influence of sinful gossip?

The Bible tells us, *"Do not conform any longer to the pattern of this world but be transformed by the renewing of your mind" (Romans 12:2). Our minds are renewed by turning away from sin in our hearts and trusting in God's very great and precious promises, so that through them [we] may participate in the divine nature and escape the corruption in the world caused by evil desires" (2 Peter 1:4)*. The Holy Spirit uses these promises to purify our hearts and to transform our lives.

Date:

I am grateful for:

_____
_____
_____
_____
_____
_____
_____

Dear Father GOD:

_____
_____
_____
_____
_____
_____
_____
_____
_____
_____
_____
_____
_____
_____
_____
_____
_____

Chapter 3
Beware of Impure Conversations

If you were a kid or a parent during the last thirty-five years, you probably remember the song "The People in Your Community "from the popular kids show. This song was a little different each time it was sung because it always introduced a new community: a policeman, a fireman, a meter reader, a baker, or a postman. The refrain went something like this: "Well, they're the people that you meet when you're walking down the street. They're the people that you meet each day." The point of the song was to help kids recognize the various kinds of people who live in their community and to know how to relate to them. It made children feel safe to know what was going on in their little world by helping them to understand the different kinds of people who populated it and how those people would generally act.

Proverbs does the same thing. The book categorizes people into somewhat exaggerated personalities so that disciples of the Lord can recognize these people when they run into them or when they themselves are acting like them. In the Proverbs it is not the policeman and the postman; it is the sluggard, the wayward wife, the hot-tempered man, the fool and at least two kinds of gossipers.

In fact, throughout the Bible, nearly every time the word "gossip" appears, it is not the verb form of the word that shows up, as in a kind of speech, but the noun form, as in a kind of person—a gossip. The Bible is more interested in the people who are doing the speaking than it is in their words. Words are important, but they are simply the fruit, the overflow, of the heart.

Gossips come in different shapes and sizes. They (we) are motivated by different things at different times. I'd like to consider five different kinds of gossiping people that we might meet (or be) in everyday life. These five are certainly not the only types of gossip that exist in this world. Our hearts are very creative in mixing up new motivations! These are just five common types driven by at least five ordinary (but ungodly) motivations. As we consider each one, we need to remember to look deeper than the behavior, into the heart of the gossip.

We should ask ourselves the following:

1. What does this gossiper want and believe?
2. What is ruling the person's heart? Who or what is he or she worshiping?
3. What king of "poisonous liquid" is in the person's "heart bottle" that is overflowing in sinful gossip?

The Bible has a remedy, an antidote, for each type of gossip. There are very great and precious promises that speak specifically to each of these hijacked hearts. When we believe, the promises our minds are renewed, de-conforms us from the world, and transforms our words and lives to please the Lord.

Gossip 1: The Informer

Proverbs says, *"A gossip betrays a confidence, but a trustworthy man keeps a secret" (11:13)*. The Hebrew word translated as "gossip" is rakil, which means "a peddler (of secrets), a huckster/hawker, a deceiver, or a spy." The English Standard Version uses the phrase "whoever goes about slandering" to translate rakil. We might use the word "informer."

Do you have someone like this in your life? Are you an informer? One of my friends calls this "the eager-eared, probing side of gossip. Sometimes, it's so secretive, I don't catch it right away. Some folks are so good at [probing that] they [simply] mention a word or two and then just analyze my expression or the stuttering." Spies know how to wheedle a story out of us.

The spy is somebody who loves to get the dirt on someone and then use that information to his or her personal advantage. At first spies may seem trustworthy, but they really are not. As we saw, Scripture says, "A gossip betrays a confidence, but a trustworthy man keeps a secret."

Don't talk to a spy, or your secrets may be the next ones to be spilled. So what is the motivation of a spy?

Power

Spies are primarily motivated by a hunger for power. There is something that a spy wants, and such a person will use your secrets and mind to get it. That hunger for power maybe born from mischievousness. He or she might just enjoy making trouble. Or the spy may like the power of knowing something that shouldn't be known or of being the first to know something.

Some spies know that they can get something they perceive as better than what they already have by trading on secret for another. We see this often with teenage girls. They trade gossip about each other to maintain power over each other in their cliques. For the spy, gossip provides the power to include and exclude.

I'm not immune to this temptation. I like to be known as someone who knows things. I enjoy the feeling and status of being "on the inside."

Incomparably Great Power

If a desire for power is your temptation, then what you really want is Jesus. The power of gossip enslaves, but the power of Christ emancipates. Satan lies about his power, but it was derived from a source other than himself, and it is waning. The devil is a defeated ruler on the way out. Jesus' power, on the other hand, is the power that brought Him back to life after He was crucified, and it is eternal and available through the Holy Spirit of God.

If a desire for power tempts you, then pray along with Paul the prayer of Ephesians 1:

I pray also that the eyes of your heart may be enlightened in order that you may know the hope in which He has called you, the riches of his glorious inheritance in the saints, and his incomparable great power for us who believe. That power is like the working of his mighty strength, which he exerted in Christ when he raised him from the dead and seated him at his right hand in the heavenly realms, far above all rule and authority, power and dominion, and every title that can be given, not only in the present age but also in the one to come. (1:18-21)

That is gospel power, and it is better than anything that gossip promises. How did Jesus use His power? He used it to love. Jesus was a "trustworthy" man. Someone to whom you could entrust your deepest most shameful secrets, and know they were as safe as can be. He still is and we can learn to be trustworthy too. (Proverbs 11:13)

Gossip 2: The Complainer

The other Hebrew word that is commonly translated as "gossip" in the Proverbs is rechilut. For example, *"A perverse man stirs up dissension, and a gossip [rechilut] separates close friends" (Proverbs 16:28)*. The English Standard Version consistently translates rechilut as "whisperer". The Hebrew dictionaries say that a rechilut is one who is murmuring about another person behind their back rather than openly complaining about their behavior. The root word for rechilut is the same word used to describe the people of Israel when they grumbled in their tents.

Did the Israelites go out and talk directly with the Lord about their concerns? No, they hid in their tents and murmured about Him in secret (Of course, He heard them: you can't really talk behind the Lord's back).

The grumbler complains. He criticizes. When she is upset about something--- and misery loves company---she will talk about others behind their backs. We often euphemistically call this "venting". Yet there is no constructive purpose in this kind of talk, and no love in the speaker's heart. Just grumbling.

Jealousy

For grumblers' jealousy is also a key factor in their motivations. A pastor friend of mine who knew I was studying gossip asked me if jealousy was the root of all gossip. It seemed to him that most if not all the gossip he encountered came out of a jealous heart. That makes sense, does it not? If you are jealous, you will be tempted to grumble behind the back of someone who has something you want: a job, a girlfriend, a house, happiness, or whatever.

Content in Any and Every Situation

The gospel remedy for grumbling is contentment and thanksgiving. It is not bad to want something, but it is terribly enslaving to want something too much. As Believers, we need to cultivate a heart of contentment with what we have and of thanksgiving for what we have been given.

Grumbling gossip feels good, even justified, and righteous. But it is not good. Contentment, however, feels even better. Contentment is counting your blessings and knowing that if you have Jesus Christ, you have everything.

The Apostle Paul knew something about contentment. He said, *"I know what it is to be in need, and I know what it is to have plenty. I have learned the secret of being content in any and every situation, whether well fed or hungry, whether living in plenty or living in want" (Philippians 4:12).*

So what was the secret of his contentment? He tells us in the next verse: *"I can do everything through Christ who gives me strength" (4:13).*

That will undo grumbling.

Gossip 3: The Backstabber

Like the grumbler, the backstabber is full of complaint, but his heart is angrier, more hateful. Backstabbing gossip overflows from a heart bent on revenge, retaliation, and real malice. The backstabber desires the target of his gossip to experience pain.

The backstabber usually begins by speaking lies, starting what we call a "smear campaign". Or a backstabber will hurt someone by simply publishing a shameful truth. Love, on the other hand, covers the warts in another's reputation. Backstabbing not only uncovers the warts but sticks a knife in them.

Absalom was a backstabber. King David's son sat at the gates of Jerusalem and complained about his dad's leadership. He told visitors pursuing lawsuits that King David had not appointed enough judges and that justice was not getting done. Absalom did not say this to David, just to the people. He wanted to steal the kingdom from his father, and he almost succeeded.

King David experienced backstabbing. Remember how he was sick in Psalm 41, and it brought out the gossip of his enemies? He said, *"My enemies say of me in malice, "When will he die, and his name perish?" ...All my enemies whisper together against me: they imagine the worst for me, saying, "A vile disease has beset him; he will never get up from the place where he lies" (41:5, 7-8).* This is hate.

Here is betrayal: *"Even my close friend, whom I trusted, he who shared my bread, has lifted up his heel against me" (41:9).* Was David talking about Absalom here? We do not know. But we do know that the Lord Jesus quoted Psalm 41:9 at the Last Supper to refer to Judas Iscariot. Our Lord too knows what it is like to be betrayed.

Malicious gossip, the kind that leads to backstabbing, is the worst kind, because it is more like Satan's behavior. Hateful gossip tears apart Churches. Paul fought it at Corinth (2 Corinthians 12:20). John dealt with it in his churches (3 John 10). Malicious gossip is a cancer. It must be stopped.

Payback

Several key motivations can be given for backstabbing. Proverbs says, *"The purposes of a man's heart are deep waters, but a man of understanding draws them out" (20:5).* Motives are often murky and difficult to discern, yet it is possible to wade through them and understand, to some degree, why we do what we do.

For many the water inside the backstabber's heart bottle is the water of revenge. The backstabber has been foiled, perhaps hurt or damaged, and is now angry. He is angry to the point at which he wants someone to pay for what has caused his pain. Gossip becomes a delicious means of payback. The target does not even know what is coming until it's too late.

Backstabbers however must beware. Gossip does not satisfy. It does not always work. Backstabbing often backfires. Wisdom found in Proverbs says, *"If a man digs a pit, he will fall into it: if a man rolls a stone, it will roll back on him. A lying tongue hates those it hurts, and a flattering mouth works ruin" (26:27-28).* And what does the gospel say to backstabbers? Certainly, more than just "Don't do it! Cut it out! Don't be a hater! As right as these rebukes might be, they don't go very deep into the heart. The gospel says to the backstabber, *"Justice will be done. Leave it in the proper hands" (Romans 12:19).*

Yes, we should pursue loving confrontation when someone has hurt us. Yes, we should take offenses to the proper authorities. But no, we are not to take revenge. God will see that justice is done. The Bible says,

Do not take revenge, my friends, but leave room for God's wrath, for it is written: "It is mine to avenge, I will repay," says the Lord. On the contrary, "If your enemy is hungry, feed him, if he is thirsty, give him something to drink. In doing this, you will heap burning coals on his head." Do not be overcome by evil but overcome evil with good. (Romans 12:19-21)

Only a Christian can overcome evil with good. We know that every wrong will be repaid either at the cross or in the eternal judgment. Knowing this changes our hearts. It makes it possible for us to not take revenge.

Gossip 4: The Pretender

A chameleon is a person who goes along with gossip to try to fit into the crowd. A commenter on a blog said, "I think that sometimes people gossip so they can be a part of the conversation. If they know something interesting about another person, they might get people to listen to them." In other words, everybody else is doing it, and we don't want to be left out.

Escaping the Snare

Fear, not anger, is the main motivation for a chameleon's gossip. A chameleon is afraid of what her peers will think, say, or do if she does not produce some gossip on demand. She is especially afraid of being excluded.

We can easily scoff at others when they are afraid in this way, but when we are the ones in a similar situation, we find that it is very difficult to resist the pressure. Proverbs says, *"Fear of man will prove to be a snare, but whoever trusts in the Lord is kept safe" (29:25).*

The key for the chameleon is to trust in the Lord and, even more, to fear Him. The Lord Jesus said, *"I tell you, my friends, do not be afraid of those who kill the body and after that can do no more. But I will show you whom you should fear. Fear him who, after the killing of the body, has power to throw you into hell. Yes, I tell you, fear him" (Luke 12:4-5).* He answers to the fear of man is the fear of God. But not a slavish fear. Jesus goes on to say, *"Are not five sparrows sold for two pennies? Yet not one of them is forgotten by God. Indeed, the very hairs of your head are all numbered. Don't be afraid, you are worth more than many sparrows" (12:6-7).* The fear of God brings peace and comfort.

Imagine a chameleon-type person hanging around with other gossipers. She has to participate in dishing out gossip because she is afraid of being excluded by the other teachers.

Let's imagine, however, that her mind becomes full of God's character, His holiness, His omnipotence, His faithfulness, His awesomeness. And let's imagine further that she reminds herself that her hairs are numbered, and that God truly cares for her.

If God looms in her mind and heart like that, her coworkers' opinions and comments will shrink in importance, and the chameleon will begin to stand out as a follower of Christ.

Gossip 5: The Troublemaker

The busybody is a person who is idle, not engaged in purposeful business and wants to be entertained. He gossips for self-satisfaction and for the purpose of living vicariously through the stories of others. A busybody enjoys meddling in other people's business. Paul says, *"They are not busy, they are busybodies" (2 Thessalonians 3:11).*

It is easy to fall into this kind of behavior. In First Timothy 5 Paul explained to Timothy what to do about widows. The church in Ephesus had a list of widows whom they supported. A widow had to meet certain qualifications to be put on the list. Most of the qualifications were about godliness, but to be added to the list, a woman also had to be an older widow, because younger widows would be prone to certain temptations, if they were put on a list like this when they were too young. Paul told Timothy, *"They get into the habit of being idle and going about from house to house. And not only do they become idler, but also gossips and busybodies, saying things they ought not to" (1 Timothy 5:13).*

Let's be clear: this behavior is not just a female thing! Women get blamed for being gossipers more than men do because they are more relational by nature and more interested in the things that make up stereotypical gossip. Gossip though, is a gender equal sin. The busybodies Paul confronted in Thessalonica included several unemployed men. If we are not busy with productive, purposeful, godly activity, any of us can easily be sacked into being a gossipy busybody.

Being a busybody gets us into trouble, especially when we get involved in people's conflicts. Proverbs says, *"Like one who seizes a dog by the ears is a passerby who meddles in a quarrel not his own" (26:17).* I wouldn't want to try grabbing the ears of the big barking dogs in my neighborhood, so why would I insert myself and my unsolicited opinions into someone else's problem? Is it because I am lacking something good to do?

Escape from Boredom

Our culture encourages it all: gossip columns, gossip shows on television, and gossip blogs with the latest story about whichever celebrity is popular this moment. Gossip is big business in show business. The entertainment industry has tapped into the desire of the masses to escape from boredom. We talk about other people to have something to do.

Can you relate? I know that I can certainly be a busybody when I'm bored. I hate to admit it, but I was hooked on general hospital when I was a teenager. That was a malignant desire to be entertained by bad stories.

We rationalize it. "It is not malicious gossip" we say. And that is true. But it isn't love either. Remember that the Lord Jesus said we would have to give an account *"for every careless word" (Matthew 12:36),* not just the malicious ones.

Almost all the reality shows on television make us feel good about ourselves. I have a new slogan that I have been preaching to myself recently, "The foolish people of the world do not exist for my entertainment.

That is a hard one to accept. We love to talk about the foolish, shameful things that people do. There are many places on the Internet that are devoted to laughing at the folly of others. Isn't that the point of thinking how stupid other people are. But that isn't how God treats people, is it? God loves people and treats them with much more mercy than they deserve. God loves me, and I have been a fool. But God in love, sent His own Son to die for fools in order to make us wise. The "gospel escape" from boredom is active love, active service, and active mercy for other people- including those who do not deserve it one bit. Paul tells the young widows to marry and to have children (see 1 Timothy 5:14). Marriage and motherhood are not an antidote to gossip, but they sure can be an antidote to idleness! Paul told the busybody men in the church in Thessalonica to get a job, and if they were not willing to do so, they were not to eat. And the rest of the church was to warn them and keep away from them (2 Thessalonians 3:10-15; also 1 Thessalonians 5:14). If we reach out to others in love, we will never be bored. Tired? Yes.

Bored? No.

The People that You Meet

So, these are some of the people in our communities: the spy, the grumbler, the backstabber, the chameleon, and the busybody. Recognize them? We have run into all of them at one time or another- and have been most of them too! These people might act differently from one another, but at heart, they are all the same. Each one is moved by a heart that believes Satan's original lie, loves a bad story and worships something that is not God. Each one has gotten everything backwards. Each one uses words to selfishly serve himself or herself rather than to love God and love other people (see Luke 10:27).

But our gracious God speaks to each of these hearts with His life-changing gospel truth, and He is speaking to each one of us right now (see Hebrews 3:7- 13). Are we listening to God about sabotaging ourselves? Now we need to understand why self-care is so important.

Date:

A List of Spiritual Blessings:

How I have seen the Hand of GOD today:

Chapter 4
Spiritual Renewal

Self-care is anything you do to take care of yourself so you can stay physically, mentally, and emotionally well.

Self-care is not synonymous with self-indulgence or being selfish. Self-care means taking care of yourself so that you can be healthy, you can be well, you can do your job, you can help and care for others, and you can do all the things you need to and want to accomplish in a day.

Self-care includes everything related to staying physically healthy — including hygiene, nutrition, and seeking medical care when needed. It's all the steps an individual can take to manage stressors in his or her life and take care of his or her own health and well-being.

The ability of individuals, families, and communities to promote health, prevent disease, maintain health, and to cope with illness and disability with or without the support of a healthcare provider.

Common examples of self-care include maintaining a regular sleeping routine, eating healthy, spending time in nature, doing a hobby you enjoy, and expressing gratitude.

There are six types of self-care: emotional, physical, social, practical, mental, and spiritual.

- Emotional Self-Care. Activities that help you connect, process, and reflect on a full range of emotions. ...
- Practical Self-Care. ...
- Physical Self-Care. ...
- Mental Self-Care. ...
- Social Self-Care. ...
- Spiritual Self Care.

It's time to Reclaim yourself! Reclaim your pen. Reclaim your dance. Reclaim your vision. Reclaim your dreams Reclaim your canvas. Reclaim your breath. Reclaim your body. Reclaim your dreams. Reclaim your voice. Reclaim your meditation. Reclaim your music. Reclaim your prayers. Reclaim your devotion. Reclaim your altar.

Reclaim the things that make you who GOD created you to be and the things that bring you to a place of peace and abide in HIM! Because gossip should never be an option! Stop it!!

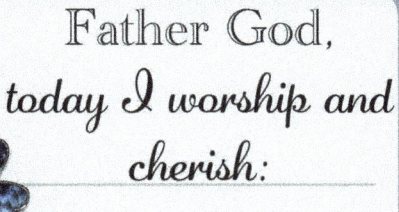

Father God, today I worship and cherish:

What are the prayer request that I should ask GOD for today?

What is GOD calling me to do today?

Chapter 5
Spiritual Renewal

Sinful Judgments

Most, if not all, sinful gossip includes the sin of judging others. When we sinfully gossip, then even before we go and bear bad news behind someone's back, our bad hearts have already passed sentence upon that person. This is true no matter what kind of gossiper we are.

The spy tries to get people to feel judgmental enough to wangle a secret out of them. The grumbler has decided in his heart that the person he is talking about is clearly wrong and merits a complaint, at least, and probably a much stronger denunciation. The backstabber is certain of her judgment and knows that her target deserves the retaliation that is on the way. The chameleon listens in on the judgments of others and does not speak up for fear of reprisal. The busybody escapes from boredom by issuing entertaining but condemning judgments about other people to his or her friends. Busybodies snicker at those they judge to be "the stupid people."

The connection between sinful judging and sinful gossip is clearly seen in the book of James:

Brothers do not slander one another. Anyone who speaks against his brother or judges him speaks against the law and judges it. When you judge the law, you are not keeping it, but sitting in judgment on it. There is only one Lawgiver and Judge, the one who can save and destroy. But you---who are you to judge your neighbor. James 4:11-12.

The Greek word translated "slander" in James 4:11 is katala-leo, and it means more than just maliciously lying about someone, which is how we tend to define the English word "slander." Kataleleo means to speak against someone, to talk them down, to speak ill of them, to disdain someone or to run someone down verbally. Older versions translate James 4:11 this way: "Speak not evil of another brethren."

Kataleleo appears right next to the chief Greek word for gossip (psithurism) in both Romans 1:30 and 2 Corinthians 12:20. Kataleleo is the larger category of evil speaking against someone and gossip itself is actually a subcategory of the word, meaning to katalaleo, or speak against someone, behind the person's back. James connects Kataleleo to sinful judging. He says, as we read above, "Brothers, do not slander, [run down, disdain, gossip about] one another." Why? He goes on: "Anyone who speaks against his brother or judges him speaks against the law and judges it." When we speak against someone in this way, James says that we are sinfully judging that person.

I said, "sinfully judging," because not all judging is sinful (just as not all small talk is sinful gossip). We have to make judgments all the time. We are called upon to make decisions about other people to access their character and reliability. The Bible calls for us to be discerning people who use good judgment.

But there is an unnecessary kind of judging that leads to sinful gossip. This is the kind of judging that Jesus talked about when He said, *"Do not judge, or you too will be judged" (Matthew 7:1)*. We call this kind of judging "judgmental," as it is more of an attitude. It's a heart disposition meant to be condemnatory and censorious.

Where do we go wrong with judging? Let's consider three main ways.

1. Rush to Judgment

I found a conclusion about Daniel before I had all the facts about his situation. This is easy to do. Proverbs says, *"He who answers before listening- that is his folly and his shame" (18:13)*. I sure felt ashamed and foolish with Daniel. I don't like to joke by pushing my luck and jumping to conclusions. It's not a joking matter, it is important for followers of Christ not to jump to conclusions.

Listening to Only One Side

Much of gossip is simply passing on one side of a story. A teacher out West wrote to me about a gossip situation in a local hospital. A woman came to work Sunday and requested prayer for a young lady in their tight-knit community. She said the young lady had been kicked out of her home by her parents, and in desperation she had moved in with her boyfriend. Everyone in the hospital felt sorry for her and started to pray for her. But that is not all there was to the story. Proverbs says, *"The first to present her case seems right, till another comes forward and questions her" (18:17)*. Yet we say, "Well, I can't exactly wait forever and talk with everyone before making a judgment!"

Actually, we can. We can suspend judgment until we have more facts. Or, at the very least, we can make a provisional judgment until we get the other side of the story. And if we do not get more of the facts, unless we are directly involved in the problem, most of the time we can live without knowing the full story.

The truth is in this case was that she left home because she wanted to live with her boyfriend, and her father had no legal recourse, because the young lady, a senior in high school, was of age. Her dad badly wanted his daughter back and was deeply grieved by the circumstances.

Before judging, get both sides.

Not Considering the Source

Hearsay and secondhand information must be treated with the ultimate care. Filling in the gaps of a story through guesswork and speculations will get us into trouble quickly. Questionable sources of information should be treated like hot uranium.

For example, beware of anything that comes to your inbox with these letters in front of it: Fwd. Just because something is on the Internet does not make it true. Sure, that should be obvious, but how many times have well-meaning people believed something they read in an anonymous e-mail and then gullibly passed it on?

Proverbs says, *"A simple man believes anything, but a prudent man gives thought to his steps" (14:15)*. Do not believe everything you hear.

Assuming Motives

You and I are not mind readers. We cannot see inside the hearts of other people and know exactly what makes them tick. Only God can do that. Therefore, we need to assume the best, not the worst, about others' motives whenever possible. Unless someone tells us, what motivates them or it has become obvious through a "pattern of incontrovertible facts that can lead to no other reasonable conclusion," we need to assume the best.

Assuming motives almost plunged Israel into civil war on one occasion. We read in Joshua 22 that after the nation had finally experienced victory and gained rest from their enemies, three of their tribes, Reuben, Gad, and Manasseh went back over the river to their previously agreed-upon home in Gilead. *The next thing they did was erect an "imposing altar" on their side of the Jordan (22:10)*.

The other tribes assembled at Shiloh to wage war. Why? They assumed that the half-tribes were setting up their own sacrificial system to rival the one in Israel. Israel had already experienced the pain of God's discipline for allowing false worship in the past. They were not going to let that happen again so soon.

Thankfully, they sent a team across the river first to try to stop the half- tribes by diplomatic means. In that heated conference it came out that the tribes of Reuben, Gad and Manasseh had only built the altar as a symbol of witness reminding both sides of their common Lord! Disaster was averted when their true motives came out.

What situations are you tempted to gossip about right now! Do you truly know the motives of those involved? Sometimes things seem obvious. After all, we read in Joshua 22 that there was an altar standing on the riverbank! But there may be another explanation for the things that we see.

Are We Supposed to Be Ostriches!

Believing the best about someone's motives does not mean that we put our heads in the sand and pretend that nothing bad is happening. No, we must call sin, sin. But we should also hold out hope and grace for people and not assume the worst about them. That is what sinful judging is at heart: assuming the worst about someone.

As Believers, it would seem that we have more reason to assume the worst about people than most. We have the doctrine of sin. We know that people often have bad motives and do bad things. But, also as believers, we are called to give

grace and hope for people and not to assign bad motives to them until necessary. The Bible says, *"Judge nothing before the appointed time; wait till the Lord comes. He will bring to light what is hidden in darkness and will expose the motives of men's hearts" (1 Corinthians 4:5).* Let's wait for Him.

If we are slower to judge others and stop sharing our judgments, how much gossip will that cut out?

2. Prideful Judgment

It gets worse. Our problem with sinful judging goes deeper than just rushing to judgment. The book of James identifies our deeper problem as pride.

He says, *"Anyone who speaks against his brother or judges him speaks against the law and judges it. When you judge the law, you are not keeping it, but sitting in judgment on it" (James 4:11).* To give some context, the law James is talking about is the law of love, the royal law of mercy that God calls His people to obey. But when you and I sinfully judge someone, we are saying, in effect, that we are above the law. We are saying that the law does not apply to us and that we can judge it. That is not the way it works.

James goes on: *"There is only one Lawgiver and Judge, the one who is able to save and destroy. But you—who are you to judge your neighbor?" (4:12).* When we find ourselves sinfully judging we are essentially playing God, so we think! Who do we think we are?

Is This My Place?

The Lord calls us to be the servants of others, but we are tempted to act as if we are their judges. Instead, when we get into these kinds of situations, we should regularly ask ourselves questions like these:

- Is this my place?
- Is this my job?
- Am I part of this situation? What part?
- Is judging this person my calling, my responsibility?

If the answers are no, then we need to cut it out.

Of course, there are positions in life in which we are temporarily required to serve as a judge. Parents have to serve as judge at times, as do teachers, coaches, and church leaders. Most earthly positions of authority come with a limited responsibility to adjudicate something.

But even in those cases, we serve as judges. We do not play God and make up our own standard, and we do not pretend that we would never do what another person has done. That's one of worst forms of judging---acting as if we ourselves have never done anything as wrong as what someone else has done, anything similarly foolish or anything every bit as worthy of condemnation. God knows better. The Lord Jesus says that we need to apply the same standard to ourselves as we do to those we are tempted to judge, because God's word says He will.

Do not judge or you too will be judged. For in the same way you judge others, you will be judged, and with the same measure you use, it will be measured to you. Why do you look at the speck of sawdust in your brother's eye and pay no attention to the plank in your own eye? How can you say to your brother, *"Let me take the speck out of your eye" when all the time there is a plank in your eye? You hypocrite, first take the plank out of your own eye, and then you will see clearly to remove the speck from your brother's eye. (Matthew 7:1-5)*

In the Same Way You Judge Others

How often do the Believers judge what is wrong with the Muslims but give their group a pass when it comes to what is wrong with them? And vice versa! Muslims find fault with the Believers over everything, yet they do not criticize their own groups. It is pride when we pick and choose what is most wrong about another based upon our own self- evaluation. We all are prone to do this.

Here is where Jesus' Golden "Rule of Thumb" is so golden. The Lord says, *"So in everything, do to others what you would have them do to you, for this sums up the Law and the Prophets." (Matthew 7:12)*. Given this command, we should consider the following:

1. How would you have others judge you?
2. With what standard?
3. With what tone?
4. With what attitude would you want to be judged?

Once you have your answers, then choose that standard, that tone and that attitude when making your judgments. Use that standard when you are talking about people who are not present.

I read the following little story in an email. I doubt that it is true (it was marked "Fwd" after all), but it makes a good point. A young couple moved into a community. The next morning while they were eating breakfast, the young woman saw her neighbor hanging the wash outside.

"That laundry is not very clean," she said. "She doesn't know how to wash correctly. Perhaps she needs better laundry soap."

Her husband looked on but remained silent. Every time her neighbor would hang her wash to dry, the young woman would make the same comments.

About one month later, the woman was surprised to see a nice clean wash on the line and said to her husband, "Look, she has learned how to wash correctly. I wonder who has taught her this."

The husband said, "I got up early this morning and cleaned our windows." The email ends, "And so it is with life. What we see when watching others depends on the window through which we look." How true!

Proverbs says, *"A man who lacks judgment derides his neighbor, but a man of understanding holds his tongue" (11:12).*

Humble Yourself

The antidote to prideful judgment is humility. In the verse right before James' condemnation of slander and judging, he says, *"Humble yourself before the Lord, and he will lift you up" (4:19).* We need to judge our judgments, check our motives and remember our place.

3. Unloving Judgment

Another name for sinful judging is critical judgment. The opposite virtue is called charitable judgment. The word "charitable" comes from the old word for love, which is charity, and it is beautifully described in 1 Corinthians 13:

Love [charity] is patient, love is kind. It does not envy, it does not boast, it is not proud. It is not rude, it is not self-seeking, it is not easily angered, it keeps no record of wrongs. Love does not delight in evil but rejoices with the truth. It always protects, always trusts, always hopes, and always perseveres. Love never fails. (1 Corinthians 13:4-8)

If you and I are loving people with this kind of charity, we won't sinfully judge or gossip about people. We won't delight in evil that we hear has befallen someone else. We won't believe the worst about others. We will always hope for something better. Love is tenacious. Love does not pretend that all is well and sweep things under the carpet, but it does hang onto hope for others and believe the best.

This is how Jesus loved us, isn't it? Substitute the name" Jesus" for the word "love" in First Corinthians 13 to see the greatest example of "The most excellent way" (1 Corinthians 12:31).

Can you imagine Jesus gossiping about us? He would surely be fully qualified to do so. He knows the whole truth about us and could rush to judgment. He is the lawgiver and the judge. Yet Jesus is patient and kind. Jesus does not delight in evil. He does not sinfully judge us. He saved us by His own sacrificial death. If Jesus has shown us this love, we need to show it to others.

Looking Ahead

Of course, it is not enough when it comes to judgmental gossip to just tell ourselves, "Cut it out!" We must learn how to do that. What do we do instead?

Date:

Father God, today I worship and cherish:

What are the prayer request that I should ask GOD for today?

What is GOD calling me to do today?

Chapter 6
The Transformation

I wish I had a dime for every time I've heard someone say, "But if we didn't gossip, we wouldn't have anything to talk about!"

Of course, that is not true. But it often feels as it is.

If you are like me, you do not want to gossip. Sure, you feel like gossiping sometimes, but your basic stance is against it. You do not want to be a gossip monger. After all, you are reading about "A Change of heart, mind, and direction." But gossip often feels irresistible. It is hard to see any alternative.

What do we do instead of gossiping?

The good news is that God wants to help us. The Lord does not want us to just stop our sinful behavior. He wants us to live righteously. And He gives us practically everything we need to do just that.

Filthy Words

In Ephesians 4 God instructs us through the Apostle Paul. He says, *"Do not let any unwelcome talk come out of your mouths, but only what is helpful for building others up according to their needs, that it may benefit those who listen"* (4:29).

The Greek word translated "unwholesome" is sapros. It means something rotten, corrupt, or decomposed. Sapros was used to talk about fruit that had gone bad and fish that had begun to stink. So, words that are sapros are rotten words. Yucky words. Words gone bad. Stinky bad news. Gossip is not the only kind of talk that fits into that category, but it is definitely in there.

Notice that Apostle Paul does not just call on the Ephesians to refrain from rotten words, but he also instructs them instead to use their words to bless others. Overcoming gossip is not just about what not to do but what to do.

And Stop It!

Become Who You Are

To really understand Ephesians 4:29 (and especially to live it out), we have to understand it in its context. In the first three chapters of Ephesians, the Apostle Paul explains the gospel as God's amazing eternal plan to bring glory to Himself through Christ. Then Apostle Paul turns a corner and applies the gospel. So, in the last three chapters of the book, he explains the implications of the gospel worked out in our lives: in a word, change. The truth of the gospel transforms us so that now we can live differently.

Before Christ we lived one way. We were, *"darkened in our understanding and separated from the life of God because of the ignorance that is in us due to the hardening of our hearts. Having lost all sensitivity, we gave ourselves over to sensuality to indulge in every kind of impurity, with a continual lust for more"* *(Ephesians 4:18-19)*. That sounds like the addictive quality of gossip, doesn't it? "A continual lust" for more of those "choice morsels."

Now we live differently. The next couple of verses explain our transformation: *"We, however, did not come to know Christ that way. Surely, we heard of him and were taught in him in accordance with the truth that is in Jesus" (4:20-21)*. That's the gospel! That's the good news about Jesus Christ and His death and resurrection and the gift of His Spirit and the promise of His return.

Apostle Paul goes on to say that we *"were taught, with regard to our former way of life, to put off our old self, which is being corrupted by its deceitful desires; to be made new in the attitude of our minds; and to put on the new self, created to be like God in true righteousness and holiness" (4:22-24)*. He is saying that our new relationship with Jesus through the gospel has changed everything. As a result, we need to become who we are. We have a new identity now, and we need to live out of that identity.

Apostle Paul compares it to changing clothes. Take off an old coat. Put on a new coat. The old coat, the old you must go. It is the *"being corrupted by its deceitful desires" (4:22)*. Instead, we need to "be made new in the attitude or our minds" (4:23). That means taking in and believing all the gospel truths we've learned so far. Moreover, we need to *"put on the new self, created to be like God in true righteousness and holiness." (4:24)*. That's the new coat! It's the real you, the you now in Christ. It is who you really are by grace. But we need to put this new self on. The Apostle Paul ran with this idea: Put off lying, Put on truth-speaking. Put off sinful anger. Put on peacemaking. Put off stealing. Put on generosity. Do you see the pattern? Put off. Put on. We could call this repenting and obeying. Doing this comes not through our self-effort but out of our faith in Christ and our new identity in Him.

This is the context for Ephesians 4:29, which says, *"Do not let any unwholesome talk including rotten gossip come out of your mouth, but only what is helpful for building others according to their needs, that it may benefit those who listen."*

Put off gossip, Put on up-building speech.

It's not a one-and-done sort of thing. It is an as-often-as needed sort of thing.

Put off. Put on. Again and again and again.

Now let's get really practical. What does this look like in real life? Let me suggest five things that we can do instead of speaking gossip- five new coats for us to put on.

1. Say Nothing At All

If you are faced with gossip or the possibility of gossiping, often the best thing to say is nothing. As the saying goes, "If you can't say anything good, don't say anything at all." Silence is golden. Proverbs says, *"When words are many, sin is not absent, but he who holds his tongue is wise" (10:19)*. Often discretion is evidenced by silence. Proverbs 17 says, *"A man of knowledge uses words with restraint, and a man of understanding is even-tempered. Even a fool is thought wise if he keeps silent, and discerning if he holds his tongue" (17:27-28)*.

President Abraham Lincoln put it this way: *"It is better to keep your mouth shut and let them think you are a fool than to open your mouth and remove all doubt."* This rule of thumb goes not just for face-to-face talking but also for texting, messaging, e-mailing and every other kind of communication through which gossip could flow.

Secrets

When I was teaching about resisting gossip in college, one of my classmates asked me an insightful question.

Is it gossip if someone confides in you about something and asks you not to tell anyone but to pray for them? You in turn have a believing friend, a prayer warrior, who you trust would never repeat anything you tell them. Is it gossip if I repeat what someone confides in me to my believing friend only for them to pray about the situation?

If someone asks you not to share something with anyone but just to pray, then you should not tell anyone and just pray. Remember, *"A gossip betrays a confidence, but a trustworthy man keeps a secret" (Prov. 11:13)*. You certainly could ask your prayer-requesting friend if you can share the secret with a safe prayer warrior who has your absolute trust, but do not do it if you have been asked not to.

I had a similar problem when I was writing this chapter. I learned of a scandalous secret, and I wanted so much to tell someone. Not someone involved- just someone, anyone! But I held my tongue and will continue to do so, because I want to be a trustworthy woman.

There are exceptions of course. For example, the case of someone being significantly harmed by keeping a secret such as a suicidal threat. This kind of information clearly should be revealed to those who can help. In fact, no secret is absolute if it will damage someone. However, most of the time, silence is golden. Apostle Paul says that "only what is helpful" should be shared. Nothing more.

2. Commend the Commendable

Often, we can do even better than silence. We can say something good. Ephesians 4:29 also tells us to speak words that are *"helpful in building up others."* That means offering encouragement, commendation, affirmation, and approving words. If we are tempted to talk about someone, then we should talk about that person's good points.

The next time you are tempted to gossip about someone, talk about how good that individual is. That is what Jesus' Golden Rule implies. Speak about people in the way you would want them to speak about you.

Commending Instead of Complaining

Have you ever heard a kid complain about his or her parents behind their backs! She may say, "My dad never lets me do anything," or, "My mom never lets us sit on the white furniture. In most cases these kinds of complaints are gossip. Instead, kids could and should honor their father and mother by saying things like, "My dad takes me places," "My mom is kind to me," "My dad is so funny. He makes me laugh". My mom is an awesome cook.

As adults, we can honor our moms and dads in the same way, even if we are older. We can also compliment our coworkers, fellow church members and neighbors even if most of the time they get on our nerves.

So, if there is absolutely nothing good to say about a person, do not say anything at all. But if there is something good, anything, then let's hear that instead. Build people up when they are not around. Bear good news about people instead of bad.

Aren't we all attracted to people who build others up? Not people who pretend that everyone is good all the time-that's false and rotten in itself. Not people who flatter others, that's false too. But people who choose not to tear others down, these people are extremely appealing. We want to be around them. We want to be like them.

Those who constantly complain, however, are revolting.

Edify!!

The old word for up-building talk is "edification." It is too bad that we've lost that word because it communicates something powerful: our words can make someone feel as solid as a rock or decimate a person the way a wrecking ball could. In Eastern College my friends and I used to jokingly bid each other, "Air head!" It was our belittling way of reminding ourselves of the potency of our words.

Edification does not mean that we commend the un-commendable. That's lying. Just find out what you can say that's positive and then build up from there. Need a few ideas? I got the phrase "commend the commendable" from Sam Crabtree's book, "Practicing Affirmation." Crabtree offers a great list of options. Because of our new identity in Christ, it is very possible to say good things about people. talk to People, not about them.

When there is a problem between us and another person, the overwhelming temptation for us is to run to just about anybody other than the one with whom we have the conflict. The way forward in conflict, however, is not to talk about the other person but to talk to the person in love. Jesus says, *"First go and be reconciled to your brother" (Matthew 5:24).*

Sometimes that's really hard to do. Yet remember, the new you that you are putting on is greater and stronger and more real than the old you. You can do it. Put off gossip and put on loving confrontation.

Did someone offend you at the gym? Talk to her about it. Did a coworker hurt your feelings in a meeting? Bring it up with her. Did your parents' recent decision mess up your plans? Take it up with them.

We need to teach this kind of loving confrontation to our kids. Does the following conversation sound familiar?

Child: "Audrey hit me!" (Bearing bad news behind Alana's back)
Mommy: "Why are you telling me this?"
Child: "To get her in trouble!"
Mommy: "You need to go talk with Audrey about that and both of you say
        sorry. If you can't resolve it, then I'll get involved."

Here is Paityn and Lailah fussing over the binky, or Cheyenne and TaYon having a sensitive moment with each other. Saraiyah and Iyima just not listening to mommy. All these situations can end with so much love, patience, and understanding. These mommies love their children so much and they all lead by loving examples.

We all need to practice loving confrontation. As we've seen. Apostle Paul says that we should speak "what is helpful for building others up according to their needs." Sometimes what people really need is loving confrontation.

I should note that it is not gossip to report a crime to the police or an unresolved conflict to your pastor or your elders. It is not gossip to get your parents involved in a situation if you do not know how to say something to a friend or if a conversation with the person who hurt you is not going well. But the general rule is "Never about, always to."

Exception: Warnings

As we said in chapter 1, there are times when we must talk about someone else and tell people about bad things in order to warn others. Warning others is a biblical principle, and not all loving warnings will be issued in front of the subject's face. In fact, they often will not be.

We still, however, must love a person even when we are warning someone else about them. While warning, we need to do everything we can to protect the person's reputation as much as possible with as much fairness and charitable judgment as we can. Again, that is what we would want others to do for us, isn't it?

We can justify just about anything, so we definitely need to make sure our warnings are necessary. We also need to make sure that they demonstrate love toward all the people concerned. It does not mean that all the people will be happy that we shared the warnings! But our conscience can be clean if we have loved as we would want to be loved.

3. Offer Words of Mercy

Our key verse for this chapter, Ephesians 4:29, ends by saying that our words should build up others *"according to their needs so that it may benefit those who listen."* The King James Version expresses the Greek even better: it says to use words that *"may minister grace unto the hearers."*

Don't you just love people who dispense grace like it's going out of style? People like that are putting on their new coats for Jesus. They "get" who they are in Christ, and they are so much fun to be around. Proverbs says, *"The lips of the righteous nourish many" (10:21)*. Doesn't that sound good?

You and I don't have to say everything we think. In fact, we can be merciful because our heavenly Father is merciful. Often, we can do better than just staying quiet or even commending the commendable. We can go the extra mile and speak words of grace. That's what God does, isn't it? Let's be like Him. Remember, Apostle Paul said that we need to *"put on the new self, created to be like God in true righteousness and holiness" (Eph 4:24)*. That means that in a potential gossip situation, we should choose the most merciful, most gracious thing we can think of to say. It will take imagination. Righteous living takes more imagination than wicked living, because it doesn't come naturally to us. But it is so much better.

If you are creative, there are many options for beneficial words. Instead of gossiping, you could:

- Tell a good story,
- Teach something useful,
- Tell a funny joke,
- Talk about the weather,
- Share the joy of your experiences,
- Or share a loving concern for someone so that you can help him or her.

Whatever you do, say something that "benefits those who listen."

Hard-edged Words

Here's another truth: our words are not always going to be nice. Apostle Paul is not urging "niceness" upon us. I'm sure that the Apostle Paul took his own advice when he wrote his letters, yet his epistles certainly contain some words that are much harder- edged than any I have ever spoken. At some point Apostle Paul even uses ridicule, irony, satire, and name calling!

This certainly does not mean that he, in his scriptural writings, violates Ephesians 4:29. There must be ways to obey Ephesians and still use remedial words that do not immediately strike somebody as edifying. (Remembering this might help to keep us from falling into the sin of judging others who don't talk just as we think they should.)

The key, I think, is that the Apostle Paul never used those hard-edged words for his own pleasure or for personal gain. Back to the condition of the heart again! He did not use hard-edged words for the kick of it. He always used those words for God, for the gospel, for the good of the church and even for his opponents, to shake them out of their complacency and hard-heartedness.

For us, though, Ephesians 4:29 is simple to apply most of the time. Simple but not easy. And possible, because of our new identity in Christ. Remember, let's put off the old man of gossip and put on the new man of mercy-giving speech.

4. Talk to and about the Lord

Finally, in Ephesian 5, Apostle Paul exhorts us to *"speak to one another with psalms, hymns, and spiritual songs. Sing and make music in your heart to the Lord, always giving thanks to God the Father for everything, in the name of our Lord Jesus Christ" (5:19-20).* When all else fails, we can always use our words to glorify the Lord. Instead of gossiping we can talk to each other, sing to one another, give thanks, share a testimony, pray, and worship with our mouths.

Moving Forward

Putting off sinful gossip and putting on grace-giving, people building, truth-loving, God-imitating, Jesus-like speech is only one side of the coin. What can we do when someone is trying to gossip to us? We will look at that in the next chapter.

Date:

I am grateful for:

Dear Father GOD:

Chapter 7
Creating a New Heart

"It's like they don't have anything else to do but gossip!"

An Evil Kind of Listening

We've all been there, haven't we? We've all been in a conversation that suddenly takes a turn to gossip, and we're not sure what to do. We've learned that listening to gossip is almost as bad as speaking it. The Bible says, *"A wicked man listens to evil lips; a liar pays attention to a malicious tongue? (Prov. 17:4).* The Message Bible paraphrases that proverb, *"Evil people relish malicious conversation: the ears of liars itch for dirty gossip."* So, there is another category of gossip in Scripture called evil listening.

Let me be clear. Not all listening is evil. The Bible commends and commands listening. The Word says, *"Everyone should be quick to listen, slow to speak and slow to become angry" (James 1:19).* Listening is important, and we are supposed to do it regularly. Sometimes we must listen even to bad news about other people when those people are not present, especially if we are in a position of authority or responsibility.

But there is listening and then there's listening.

There is an evil kind of listening that receives gossip wickedly, and the difference, as we might expect by now, comes down to the heart. How we are listening is determined by why we are listening. The key is to listen in love. In Ephesian 5 we read, *"Be imitators of God, therefore, as dearly loved children and live a life of love, just as Christ loved us and gave himself up for us as a fragrant offering and sacrifice to God" (Eph. 5:1-2).* Our listening should be governed by Christ-like love.

Light and Darkness

There will be times when we must stand apart from those who are engaging in sinful gossip because it is not loving. Ephesians 5 calls us, as *"children of light."* Not to partner with those who are still in the darkness.

For you were once in darkness, but now you are light in the Lord. Live as children of light... Have nothing to do with the fruitless deeds of darkness, but rather expose them. For it is shameful even to mention what the disobedient do in secret. But everything exposed by the light becomes visible, for it is light that makes everything visible. (5:8, 11-13).

Not partnering with unbelievers doesn't mean not to be friends with them or not to spend time with them. It means not to take part in what they take part in if it is wicked. Even by just listening, we can find ourselves partnering with the darkness.

So, what do we do instead? Let's consider four biblical strategies for living as children of the light.

1. Pray and Weigh

I wish I could offer a simple formula for escaping gossip. When I started my research on this book, I was hoping to find a one-size fit all approach that could be automatically deployed. But life is messier than that, and God's wisdom is better than that too.

Some Bible teachers and authors give the impression that whatever gossip starts to flow, the only proper response is a hand-raised, palm-outward sanctimonious announcement: "Stop!" This conversation is now gossip, and I will not be party to it," as if we, as Believers, are called to be the gossip police.

There surely is a time for confrontation, especially among fellow believers, but there are several biblical strategies that a believer can utilize to assist in these scenarios-not just one. In fact, it is important to consider the many factors at play in your particular situations:

- What, really is going on here?
- What is my relationship to the person talking?
- What is my relationship to the person being talked about?
- How serious is this gossip?
- Is it a lie? Is it true? Is it just a rumor?
- What effects might this story have on others?
- Is this just a funny thing someone did, or is it really shameful?
- Why is this story being told? What clues do I have for assessing the motives of the speaker?
- Is this the focus of the conversation, or are things going to just flow right on?
- Does this conversation fit the description of bearing bad news behind someone's back out of a bad heart?

The Spirit of Wisdom

When faced with gossip, we need wisdom and discernment to know how to respond. Thankfully, we are not alone in the world. Children of the light have the Holy Spirit living within them- *"the Spirit of wisdom and revelation, so that you may know him better." (Eph. 1:17b).* The Spirit loves to give us the wisdom we need-we just need to ask Him for it. The Bible promises, *"If any of you lacks wisdom, he should ask God, who gives generously to all without finding fault, and it will be given to him" (James 1:5).* We need to dig for wisdom as well in the Bible *(Proverbs 2:3-5).* "*Indeed, if you call out for insight and cry aloud for understanding, and if you look for it as for silver and search for it as for hidden treasure, then you will understand the fear of the Lord and find the knowledge of God."* We can ransack our copies of the Scripture to guide us when we get into these gossip situations.

So, my first piece of advice is to pray and weigh.

1. Praying

When the conversation at work starts to go down a dark path, we should shoot up a signal flare prayer. "Lord, Help!" Help me to discern right now what to do."

We should have an inner dialogue going on with the Lord all the time. The Bible tells us to *"pray continually" (1Thes. 5:17)*. This means that our hearts should be on speakerphone with our Lord. Call Him up in the morning, and don't hang up all day. Especially in those times and situations when we think we might be getting into trouble, we need to get the Lord on the line right away. A simple "Father, help! Please give me your wisdom." The Lord loves to answer prayers like that. Often, we don't have the wisdom we need because we don't ask in prayer (James 4:2).

Weighing

After we pray, and as we are listening for God's answer, we need to weigh carefully what we hear. Proverb says, *"The heart of the righteous weighs its answer, but the mouth of the wicked gushes evil" (15:28).* This is one of those things before you speak proverbs. The wicked person ponders, considers, and weighs what he or she is about to say before saying it. As people talk to us, we need to weigh what's being said in our minds.

As we learned in chapter 4, we need to be careful not to fall into judging. Don't jump to conclusions. Get both sides. Consider the source. Suspend judgment. Weigh things out.

The Bible calls us to be discerners. Discerning the reality of a situation doesn't always take long. Often we don't have to pray or tarry for a long time in order to decide what is going on. In fact, most of the time we do it on the fly. I have a friend who gets anonymous phone calls in the middle of the night. On the other end of the line, there is always a voice telling her something bad about her husband. It doesn't take a long time to weigh in on this. The only good thing for her to do in that situation is to hang up and maybe get a trace on the call to stop the harassment.

If something we are told does begin to seem like gossip, then we must take action and not just passively receive what's being told to us.

2. Avoid

Proverbs says, *"A gossip betrays a confidence, so avoid a man who talks too much" (20:19)*. That's pretty straightforward. Don't go near a gossiper. Walk on the other side of the street. Get away from that person. You and I might need to skip out on some social situations if we know that all we will hear in them is sinful gossip. It might be a sacrifice, but it might also be worth it.

This proverb also applies to that gossip columns, gossip television show, gossip blog, gossip magazine, gossip channel and gossip Facebook page. Those things are no good for our souls and we need to avoid them like the plague. If you are addicted to them, get help, get accountability, and start flushing them out of your system today.

Shepherding Your Conversation

Sometimes we cannot avoid a person who gossips, simply because of our relationship to them. For instance, I cannot just avoid the lady's locker room and shower at home. Sometimes I need to be there because I have an appointment immediately after my Zumba workout session.

We are often placed in these kinds of situations in order to influence people for Christ. We all know individuals who are part of social circles which people easily fall into gossip. Yet as Believers, we are called to be salt and light, to strategically infiltrate those social circles. We don't become like the darkness, but we do love those who are not yet light.

In cases like these, I think we need to avoid not the person but the topic. We need to redirect conversations, if we can, to avoid the gossip in them. I suggest that when conversations turn to fault, simply change the subject. Change the theme of the conversation.

That may sound a little sneaky, but it is just shepherding a conversation and acting as a leader. The Bible says, *"Without wood a fire goes out; without gossip a quarrel dies down" (Proverbs 26:20)*. Just removing the gossip can change the temperature in a room.

3. Covering

Proverbs says, *"Whoever loves a quarrel loves sin; whoever builds a high gate invites destruction. (17:19)*. The opposite of gossip is "covering." Proverbs 10 also says, *"Hatred stirs up dissension, but love covers over all wrong" (10:12)*. What does it mean to "cover over wrongs"?

It does not mean to pretend something isn't happening or to sweep something under the rug. The Bible in no way gives perpetrators of crimes a blank check. Sin surely needs to be confronted. Proverbs is talking, however, about people who are uninvolved in the matter overlooking the offense. "Covering" means covering over a wrong, drawing a veil over it so that those who do not need to see it never do.

Covering Noah

After Noah came out of the ark in Genesis 9, he praised God and worshiped then he grew a vineyard and got plastered. Genesis says, *"He became drunk and lay uncovered inside his tent" (9:23).*

Would it have been wrong for Noah's sons to see their father in his folly?

Maybe, maybe not. Regardless, two faithful sons went the extra mile to avoid seeing it, and they were clearly commended for doing so. They honored their father even when he was being dishonorable. They covered his offense.

We can do that for other people. Not to make an excuse for them, but in order to cover over their shame so that their sin is not exposed to people, places, or things it need not be.

One evening I went out with some close friends and our conversation turned to some mutual acquaintances who are also in pastoral ministry. My friend and I knew something bad about the other pastor couple that the missionary couple did not, and I really struggled to decide how much to say and how much to hold back.

I liked and trusted the missionary couple, so it would have been easy for me to say too much. But I opted for sharing very little in an attempt to cover the other couple's disgrace. I was honest and forthright, but I did not share more than they needed to hear.

Many times, at a social gathering someone will get just far enough into a story to have everyone's attention and then say, "You know, I really shouldn't be telling you this." And of course, the listeners all respond, oh, come on, you can't stop now. We won't tell!" It would be refreshing to hear someone respond instead, "Good for you. Don't tell." I admire your self-control." We need to do what we can to stop negative talk before it gets spread.

Good idea!

Sometimes it's as simple as using body language. We can say a lot with our nods, our nudges, and winks. Don't encourage gossip with your eyebrows.

Defending as Covering

I think this kind of covering includes defending someone's reputation, as well, especially if we know a story is false.

Sometimes the right thing to do is to say, "I'm not sure about that, but I don't think that is any of our business." That's a loving rebuke, and it is covering over wrongs.

4. Go

Sometimes the best thing to do is to go directly to the one being talked about. If you think you need to know whether the story is true, go directly to that person. This is even more important if the person has sinned against you. Our Lord says, *"If your brother sins against you, go and show him his fault, just between the two of you. If he listens to you, you have won your brother over"* (Matt. 18:15).

Go Together

If someone starts complaining to you about someone else, it is good to ask the complainer if he or she has talked about the problem directly with the subject of his or her complaint. You can say, "Have you talked with the person about this? I am willing to go with you to help and to witness, but I don't think I should listen to anymore until we've gone together." This can get messy, and it's not always fun. In a world that is still covered with darkness, light and darkness tend to fight against each other. But it is definitely worth it to deal with the problem.

A friend of mine, who is an associate pastor. Soon after starting her new role, heard two strong leaders in the church speak very negatively about the lead pastor. She immediately confronted these two and challenged them to go with her to the lead pastor to talk it out.

She said, "While I wondered if this would cost me, I can say two years later that one of those women is now a supportive leader who demonstrated humility and a willingness to speak directly and honestly to our lead pastor when she had disagreements with him. The other leader is not as supportive but is under control." It isn't very easy, but her willingness to go with these women dynamically changed the situation.

Go Alone

Sometimes the other person will not go with you. So, in some cases, because it is loving to tell a person that others are gossiping about him or her, you'll need to go alone. Do this as carefully as you can. Try not to gossip about the person who has been gossiping? Use the strategies we've learned in the previous chapters. Give as much of a sympathetic ear to the comments, as much as possible, and be gracious. But if a person's reputation is being significantly harmed, it is loving to let the target know what you have heard and then to pray with them that the situation can be straightened out.

Date:

A List of Spiritual Blessings:

How I have seen the Hand of GOD today:

Chapter 8
A Heart Renewed to Jehovah

You will be gossiped about. If it has not happened yet, get ready, because someday you will find yourself in the crosshairs of the sin of gossip.

Joseph is a believer who owns rental property and tries to be just and merciful in managing it. But he had one tenant, who refused to pay his rent on time and who let the balance of unpaid debt pile up. The renter claims to be a believer, but instead of apologizing for his debt and paying up, he went through the community attacking Joseph's character. Word slowly trickled back to Joseph of what the renter was saying about him to business owners, neighbors, and friends. It hurt Joseph a lot.

What would you do if you were in Joseph's shoes? Are you ready to respond to gossip when you are its target?

Sadly, most of the time you will not know that you are a target of someone's hurtful words. Detrimental, gossip is done behind our backs, when we are not looking, when we are not listening and when we are not present. So, what do you do if, like Joseph, you get wind of what is being said about you?

Before we can learn how to relate to the other people who have become involved in these situations, especially the ones who have perpetrated the wrong against us, we need to start with how we can relate to God when we find ourselves the target of gossip.

Songs of Experience

The Psalms are the richest quarry to mine in the Bible for learning how to righteously survive being the victim of other people's sins. The Psalms are songs of experience; the one we are about to read relates the experience of being attacked, chased, hatred, slandered and of just about every other way of being sinned against! King David, especially, lived most of his life under attack, and his prayers provided to us songs in scripture. This gives us patterns to practice in our own lives today.

Psalm 140 is one of David's songs of experience. In it David sings about a time when he lived as a target of gossip. As you read it, take careful note of how he talks to God:

Rescue me, O Lord, from evil men; protect me from men of violence, who devise evil plans in their hearts and stir up war every day. They make their tongues as sharp as a serpent's; the poison of vipers is on their lips. "Selah"

Keep me, O Lord, from the hands of the wicked; protect me from men of violence who plan to trip my feet. Proud men have hidden a snare for me; they have spread out the cords of their net and have set traps for me along my path. "Selah"

O Lord, I say to you. "You are my God." Hear, O Lord, my cry for mercy. O Sovereign Lord, my strong deliverer, who shields my head on the day of battle-do not grant the wicked their desires. O Lord do not let their plans succeed, or they will become proud. "Selah"

Let the heads of those who surround me be covered with the trouble their lips have caused. Let burning coals fall upon them; may they be thrown into the fire, into miry pits, never to rise. Let slanderers not be established in the land; may disaster hunt down men of violence.

I know that the Lord secures justice for the poor and upholds the cause of the needy. Surely the righteous will praise your name and the upright will live before you. (140:1-13)

Why Gossip Hurts

Before we dissect Psalm 140, we should think a little more about why being gossiped about is bad. What makes it so hard and so painful? It is a unique form of suffering, to be sure.

First, gossip is betrayal. It is a form of treason. A close friend, someone we trust, turns out to be the one bearing the bad news behind our back. King David experienced this kind of betrayal.

In Psalm 55 he said,

If an enemy were insulting me, I could endure it; if a foe were raising himself against me, I could hide from him. But it is you, a man like myself, my companion, my close friend, with whom I once enjoyed sweet fellowship as we walked with the throng as the house of God. (55:12-14)

Next, while betrayal always hurts, it can also leave us feeling vulnerable. It's easy to become fearful when we do not know what is being said about us. At one time we may have thought that all was well, but then we find out that there is unseen chatter going on around us, and we cannot control it.

Are you feeling that right now? If you have recently found out that you are the target of gossip, you might be feeling helpless and out of control. To not know what is being said about us, much less to be able to control it, is scary.

In Psalm 55 David sings about that:

My heart is in anguish within me: the terror of death assails me. Fear and trembling have beset me: horror has overwhelmed me, I said, "Oh, that I had the wings of a dove! I would fly away and be at rest- I would flee far away and stay in the desert.... I would hurry to my place of shelter, far from the tempest and storm." (55:4-8)

David is saying that if he could have run away and hid, he would have. And he was the king! How much more can you and I feel scared and intimidated by sinful gossip?

Perhaps the most painful aspect of being gossiped about is the feeling of loss at the theft of our reputation. Let me ask you a trick question: is it good to care about our reputation? Don't answer too quickly! Is it good to value your good name?

The answer is yes.

Proverbs 22 says, *"a good name is more desirable than great riches: to be esteemed is better than silver or gold" (22:1). A good reputation is a blessed and valuable thing. A good name is something we should want and something we ought to cultivate, as much as it is in our control to do so. We should cultivate our reputations not through marketing, public relations or manipulating people's opinions of us but by being a man or woman of good character. Proverbs link a good name to wisdom. A wise man or woman will earn a good reputation.*

But gossip often robs our reputations. Shakespeare captured that thought in his play Othello:

Good name in man and woman, dear my lord.
Is the immediate jewel of their souls (sounds like Proverbs 22:1) Who steals my purse steals trash, 'tis something, nothing;
"twas mine, 'tis his, and has been slave to thousands, But he that filches from me my good name
Robs me of that which not enriches him And makes me poor indeed."

So, what do we do when we find ourselves lamenting the loss of our good name? Let's go back to Psalm 140.

1. Go Before the Lord

Notice where David goes when he gets into trouble. He says, *"Rescue me, O Lord, from evil men; protect me from men of violence, who devise evil plans in their hearts and stir up war every day" (140:1-2).* David takes his situation to the Lord first and foremost, and we should as well.

We don't tend to go to the Lord first though, do we? We take things into our own hands. We complain about those who are complaining about us. And we run around attempting to set the record straight. When we take it to the Lord, we can experience freedom and joy.

Tell It Like It Is

Notice how David cried out to the Lord in the beginning of Psalm 140. His requests were specific: *"Rescue me! Protect me!"* He talks to God about how his situation feels, and he does not mince words. *"They make their tongues as sharp as a serpent's, the poison of vipers is on their lips" (140:3)*, David goes on to say. In other words, "Lord these gossipers talk like snakes! They bite. Their words are full of poison. They speak Satan's language. Help!"

Do not be afraid to tell God how it is. God is not looking for us to just grin and bear things stoically, without feeling. Not at all! God invites us to tell Him exactly how we feel:

"Lord, I feel attacked."
"Lord, I feel betrayed."
"Lord, I feel scared."
"Lord, I feel angry."
"Lord, I hate being gossiped about!"
"Lord, take it away!"

Verse four of Psalm 140 says, *"Keep me, O Lord, from the hands of the wicked; protect me from men of violence who plan to trip my feet" (140:4).* David probably had it worse than you or I ever will. He had enemies who truly wanted him dead. Most of those who gossip about you and me don't actually want us to be killed, but the principle for us is the same as it was for David: take it to the Lord.

David continues his plea: *"Proud men have hidden a snare for me; they have spread out the cords of their net and have set traps for me along my path" (140:5).* He's essentially saying, "This is not easy, Lord! I don't like it. I'm going to trip. I'm going to fall."

Faith does not minimize our suffering. Faith does not say, "It's no big deal." Faith does not pretend that a situation is not painful or scary. What faith does do is take our problem to the One who really cares and can do something about it.

Remember You are Talking to Jehovah

David's prayers were based on his relationship with God. As he continues his prayer, he says, *"O Lord, I say to you, "You are my God." Hear, O Lord, my cry for mercy. O Sovereign Lord do not grant the wicked their desires, O Lord; do not let their plans succeed" (140:6-8).* David was not just asking some-god-out-there to do something for him. He was asking his God, the God with whom he was in covenant, the God to whom he belonged, David had already seen God work on his behalf. He is saying, "You have been there for me before, Lord, my strong deliverer. You have shielded my head in the day of battle. I know that You will be there again." I don't know all the times that people have gossiped about me. I can guess that there have been many of them. I am a public figure in our little community and have been connected to various conflicts between people in my years of ministry. I surely deserve some of the gossip shared about me. Not that people should have shared the bad news about me, but the truth is, some of the bad news was true. I am a sinner and I have failed.

But throughout all the gossip that I know has been shared about me- and some of it has been deeply painful- God has protected me, my reputation and my ministry over and over again. I am absolutely thankful for that, and it helps me to be ready to take my challenges to the Lord next time. God has always shielded my head in the day of battle, so why wouldn't I turn to Him every time?

2. Ask Yeshua for Justice

David asked God to change the plans of the wicked. In fact, he asked for a reversal- that the bad things his enemies wanted for David would come back on their heads. David wanted justice:

Do not grant the wicked their desires, O Lord, do not let their plans succeed, or they will become proud. "Selah"

Let the heads of those who surround me be covered with the trouble their lips have caused. Let burning coals fall upon them; may they be thrown into the fire. Into miry pits, never to rise. Let slanderers not be established in the lands; may disaster hunt down men of violence. (140:8-11).

David and the other psalmists asked for justice again and again. They even asked that their reputations be protected. "Protect my reputation" is not a bad prayer. For example, Psalm 71 says, *"In you, O Lord, I have taken refuge; let me never be put to shame" (71:1).* That means, in effect, "Let me not look bad in the eyes of others. Protect my reputation. Not, ultimately, for myself but for You, Lord. But do not let my reputation be unjustly bad. Bring justice, O Lord!"

Have you prayed for justice in your situation? If someone has gossiped about you and everyone seems to believe what that person has said, take the problem to the Lord, and ask Him for justice.

Two Difficult Things at the Same Time

You may, at first, have a hard time reconciling the psalmists' cries for justice with our Lord teaching us to love our enemies. You may not yet be able to pray Psalm 140:10 *"Let burning coals fall upon them: may they be thrown into the fire, into miry pits, never to rise"-* without bitterness and personal hate. It may even seem impossible for you to pray like that while at the same time holding out mercy for those who would repent. However, it is possible.

It takes becoming like Jesus, who is uniquely able to do two difficult things at the same time. I believe that if David's snake-tongued enemies had turned around and genuinely asked for forgiveness, David would have granted it gladly. David was famous for flashing hot with anger but also for dispensing grace. In that, he was like his gracious Lord.

But the Lord is not just gracious. He is also holy and just, which means retribution for the unrepentant. God is both, not either/or.

So, ask for justice while still loving your enemies. Through His work on the cross, Jesus did that, and made it possible for us to do it too. His sacrifice satisfied the demands of justice while simultaneously dispensing mercy.

If the person who gossiped about you comes and asks for your forgiveness, give it. Quickly. Freely. Joyfully. Justice will still be done. Justice will always be done. So do not be afraid to forgive, and do not be afraid to humbly ask God to bring justice to your cause.

3. Believe that the Lord Will Answer

In the last line of Psalm 140, David sings in confident faith, *"I know that the Lord secures justice for the poor and upholds the cause of the needy. Surely the righteous will praise your name and the upright will live before you" (140:12-13)*. David knew that God would answer his requests. He knew things would work out rightly. He knew God would bring justice.

Consistently, the message of the Psalms is this: *"Cast your cares on the Lord and he will sustain you, he will never let the righteous fall" (55:22)*. God will settle the score. God will see that justice is done for those who cry out for it. Your reputation will be saved! You may have to wait for it to happen.

We live in an instant society in which we expect things to happen now, on our timetable. One of my favorite corny jokes says that scientists have invented a microwave fireplace- Americans can now have a relaxing evening in front of the fire in only eight minutes. Just as in other areas of our lives, we want our justice served right away.

But God's timetable and ours are not the same. One of my pastor friends likes to say, *"God is seldom early but never late."* Similarly, in Psalm 37, David says,

Be still before the Lord and wait patiently for him; do not fret when men succeed in their ways, when they carry out their wicked schemes.

Refrain from anger and turn from wrath; do not fret-it leads only to evil. For evil men will be cut off, but those who hope in the Lord will inherit the land.

A little while, and the wicked will be no more; though you look for them, they will not be found. But the meek will inherit the land and enjoy great peace. (37:10-11)

You might have to wait a little while, but you can trust God to bring justice.

You can trust God with your reputation.

Good, not God

Remember our trick question?

Is it good to care about your reputation?

Well, here's another answer to the question: "No, Not very much."

A good reputation is valuable, but it is not worth worrying about. Again, Psalm 37 says, *"Do not fret about it- it leads only to evil" (37:8)*. Worrying about our reputation can take something good and make it a god, an idol. Idols are cruel taskmasters. They demand much and deliver little. Don't let yourself care too much about your reputation.

The Lord, Our Security

The time it takes before God comes to our defense may feel longer than we can bear. After the Lord Jesus died, God made things all right again. Jesus was vindicated by His resurrection (1 Tim 3:16). For you and I, it might get worse before it gets better. But know this, it will get better! God has promised justice. His very character brings justice and restores reputations, making everything right.

When we are gossiped about, Jesus understands. If David understood what it meant to be under attack, how much more does Jesus understand. Psalm 140 ends powerfully: *"Surely the righteous will praise your name and the upright will live before you" (140:13).*

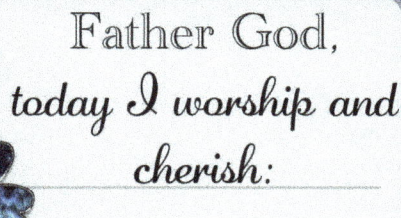

Date:

Father God, today I worship and cherish:

What are the prayer request that I should ask GOD for today?

What is GOD calling me to do today?

Chapter 9
Receptive Heart

One pastor lost his job because of gossip. A disaffected woman in a Maryland church he had pastored started complaining about him to her small group and later, to the church elders. She did not like some of the things he said from the pulpit nor how he came across personally. Some wise people suggested that she take her concerns directly to him. She refused and kept on talking about him to others. Despite nothing being said openly, a negative opinion about him spread like gangrene throughout the church.

Instead of pushing for reconciliation, the elder board listened to the gossip. They decided to force the pastor to resign. When it became obvious to the pastor that he would not get to face his accuser and that he had no support from the leadership, he left the church quietly, confused, and hurting.

Watching this sad situation unfold from a distance, I was impressed by how he responded in the face of gossip. He trusted God with his reputation, even more, he loved his enemies. Though hurt by the betrayals, he never lashed back at his opponents. He never took the gossiping route himself. He continued (and continues today) to seek reconciliation. He prayed for the church. He responded in kindness and grace. He acted like Jesus.

Love My Enemies

What do you do with an enemy?

When someone gossips about you, he or she is acting as your enemy. That person may not be your enemy in any official way. He or she may, in fact, be your closest friend. But at the moment when bad news is being spread behind your back out of a bad heart, the person doing the spreading is acting as your enemy.

So again, I ask, what do you do with an enemy? Our Lord Jesus has the answer:

You have heard that it was said, "Love your neighbor and hate your enemy." But I tell you: Love your enemies and pray for those who persecute you, that you may be sons of your Father in heaven. He causes his sun to rise on the evil and the good and sends rain on the righteous and the unrighteous. If you love those who love you, what reward will you get? Are not even the tax collectors doing that? And if you greet only your brothers, what are you doing more than others? Do not even pagans do that? (Matthew 5:43-47)

In what we call His Sermon on the Mount, Jesus teaches us to love our enemies. In this particular section of the sermon, the Lord had been masterfully correcting misunderstandings and perversions of the law of God. The law of Christ sets forth both a correct interpretation of the law and His own divinely authoritative statements. Verse 43 notes the sixth time in this sermon that Jesus said, "You have heard that it was said," and the Lord countered this saying each time with something very different from what the people had heard before. What Jesus countered with is extremely different from what we hear now in our culture as well. Not to mention from what other religions say and even from what our instincts might lead us to believe and do.

Especially this one: love your enemies.

That certainly does not come naturally to us!

Leviticus does say, *"Love your neighbor as yourself" (19:18)*. But the teachers of Jesus' day assumed that it meant, "Love your countryman, your brethren, your tribesmen." In turn, they believed that they must "hate your enemy." But the law never says, "Hate your enemy." So, Jesus counters, *"But I tell you: Love your enemies and pray for those who persecute you" (Matthew 5:44)*.

Loving someone does not mean that we have to like them. Think about the last person whom you know gossiped about you. Do you have that person in your mind's eye?

Jesus is calling you to love that individual. Not love as in some touchy-feely, warm-and-fuzzy kind of thing. Not affection but love as in actively seeking someone's good. Love is an action, primarily, not a feeling. It seeks the good of another. It involves the heart but does not equate to liking someone or approving of what they do. Let's see just how active love is:

Love is patient, love is kind. It does not envy, it does not boast, it is not proud. It is not rude, it is not self-seeking, it is not easily angered, it keeps no record of wrongs. Love does not delight in evil but rejoices with the truth. It always protects, always trusts, always hopes, and always perseveres. Love never fails. (1 Cor. 13:4-8)

We are to show active love not just toward our friends but also toward our enemies.

Just Like Our Father

When we love actively, we show our family resemblance to Jesus. Jesus said, *"Love your enemies and pray for those who persecute you, that you may be sons of your Father in heaven" (Matt 5:44-45a)*.

We know from what Jesus says elsewhere that we cannot become a son of God by being good. We cannot earn our way into sonship. We can, however, grow into our sonship by acting more and more like Jesus. This is in line with our new relationship with God and demonstrating that we are His children. I look like my earthly father. His face and mine look very similar. I'm glad I look like my father because it shows people that we are especially related to one another. Likewise, when Jesus tells us to love our enemies and we obey Him, we show the world that we are like our heavenly Dad. God sends the sun and rain not just on His friends but on His enemies. He is kind and gracious to all. Even the evil tax collectors of Jesus' day and the organized crime bosses and drug dealers of our day love those who love them and greet those who greet them. There's nothing special or Godlike about that. Loving your enemies, that's something entirely different.

Different Strokes for Different Folks

Loving an enemy looks different in each situation. As I said before about resisting gossip, there is no one formula or three-step plan that works in every situation. Your response depends upon a lot of factors. For example, what kind of gossip did someone speak about you? Sure, all gossip is sinful, but there is a big difference between idle chat shared by people you do not know and a malicious betrayal by a best friend. You will handle each case differently.

A few years ago, my friend informed me that someone had been gossiping about me. Apparently, the gossiper felt scandalized by advice I had given to a mutual acquaintance. I was told about her actions. In chapter 6 we learned, always go to the source of the gossip. The Bible tells us to be wary of our enemies. Yet we're still supposed to love them.

She is a woman in the community whom I am not sure I could point out in a lineup. I thanked my friend for the information, but it hardly changed a thing regarding the way in which I related to the woman. I might be a little more cautious of her than before, but that's okay. Each situation we come across will call for discernment, prayer, and sometimes wise counsel from other Believers. I needed to love her in spite of the gossip, but hate is never an option.

Practically speaking, what are our options? Here are four biblical love-in-action responses to use when we find ourselves the target of gossip.

1. Pray

Again, Jesus said, *"Love your enemies and pray for those who persecute you" (Matt 5:44-45a).* That is easy to say but difficult to do. When someone hurts us, it is hard for us to ask God to help that person. It is one thing if the individual talked about us behind our back, then wised up and came to us for forgiveness. But if we find out about the gossip some other way, loving prayers might be difficult to say.

If you are having trouble praying for your enemies, think about Jesus. Think about His prayers for Judas and for those who tortured and killed Him on the cross. Meditate on Jesus' prayers for us before we were reconciled to Him. When we were still His enemies, Jesus prayed, *"Father, I want those (not yet my* children) to be with me" (John 17:24). Amazing! Jesus provides us with a perfect example of loving our enemies.

What should we pray for exactly? Pray for justice, as we saw to do in the last chapter. Pray that our gossiping enemy's evil plans will backfire. But also pray for conviction and repentance and eventual blessings for our enemy. Sometimes if we pray for someone before confronting him or her, we'll find the person humbled and ashamed of his or her behavior and possibly willing to seek reconciliation. We'll find that God has already been working on that person's heart.

Pray also for yourself. Pray that you will have wisdom to know how to relate to the person who has hurt you so deeply. I suggest Paul's prayer in Philippians Chapter 1 as a great model to follow in asking God for smart love:

And this is my prayer: that your love may abound more and more in knowledge and depth of insight, so that you may be able to discern what is best and may be pure and blameless until the day of Christ—to the glory and praise of God. (1:9-11)

2. Overlook

The Bible says, *"A man's wisdom gives him patience; it is to his glory to overlook an offense" (Prov. 19:11).* Ninety percent of the time, the right thing to do when we are the target of gossip is to simply overlook the offense.

Whether we should overlook an offense or not depends upon a number of factors including,

(1) what kind of gossip it is
(2) whether the story is true or false
(3) whether it is a secret you asked someone to keep but they shared it anyway and;
(4) the seriousness of the shared information.

A great deal of gossip is just people sharing their bad opinions of us. In many of those cases, we can just overlook what they said and act as though the gossip did not happen. One of my friends says, "I'm glad when people gossip about me. At least they aren't talking about someone else!"

Overlooking is a kind of one-sided forgiving. It means that we just go on relating to the person in the same way we always did. In this case that is what I did.

Overlooking does not minimize our pain. Gossip still hurts us, but overlooking an offense is a way to absorb the pain and to move on in love. I think it is cool that God has given us this glorious option for extending grace. Overlooking saves us a lot of time and trouble in our relationships and grows us into the patient image of God.

3. Confront the Gossiper

We cannot always overlook an offense. Love may call us to confront it, especially when the problem is between brothers and sisters in Christ. Jesus said, If your brother sins against you, go and show him his fault, just between the two of you. This is another reminder that we should not go behind a person's back and gossip about his sin against us to someone else! Further steps, if necessary, will include more people in a very wise and careful way.

Love doesn't just sweep things under the rug. Love goes to the person who is acting as an enemy and shows that person his or her fault so that relationship can be restored.

I mentioned in the introduction to this book a painful time in my pastoral ministry when harmful gossip about me was at its worst and I seriously thought about quitting the pastorate. There was one couple in particular who was spreading the bad news. When I found out about it, I approached them privately and confronted them in love. On the spot these people agreed that they had sinned, and they asked for my forgiveness! Our brotherhood was restored and even improved. We are better friends now than ever before.

Sometimes people will repent, and we can experience total forgiveness and reconciliation with them. At other times they will not repent, and we will need to be patient and to forebear with them. In those instances, we need to release any bitterness we have, be ready to forgive them and continue toward reconciliation.

Question Before Confronting

Keep a few questions in mind before you confront someone who has been gossiping about you.

Is it true? Maybe the person you want to confront should not be sharing certain information about you but is the bad news a true story? Is there even a kernel of truth to it? Can you see why someone might have said it? Believers should look at more than one side of an issue. We need to be humble and to consider what part we may have played in a conflict.

If the bad news about you is not true, and it is something shameful, then make sure that it does not become true. Make sure that you do not prove your critics right by the way you live. Peter said that Christ followers should keep *"a clear conscience, so that those who speak maliciously against your good behavior in Christ may be ashamed of their slander" (1 Peter 3:16)*. Do not live their story about you. Live the gossip down.

What can I learn from this? We can profit from just about any criticism we receive; even the good, the bad, and the ugly. Just because our enemies are in the wrong does not mean that there isn't something we can learn from being talked about. God often provides good lessons for us that come from the unlikeliest of sources.

Pastors and other church leaders often miss this principle. We focus on the fact that someone is gossiping about us. "They are going about it all wrong." Yet sometimes we need to listen, even if the message is off kilter. Because of who we are in Christ, we have nothing to lose.

Of course, some backstabbing gossip is so malicious that the only thing we can learn from it is beware. Here are a few more questions to consider when planning to confront someone.

Should I defend myself? There are times when you should defend yourself and your reputation. In the book of Acts and in the New Testament letters, Peter and Apostle Paul sometimes defended their actions and sometimes did not. Their decision was determined by if they had anything to gain. Consider, would defending myself in this situation be loving? Then the Lord will direct your steps as you trust in Him.

Can I rejoice in this? If the gossip is untrue and it has come about because we are following the Lord Jesus, then God says that we should actually rejoice!

I learned to follow the Lord's instruction: *"Blessed are you when people insult you, persecute you and falsely say all kinds of evil against you because of me. Rejoice and be glad, because great is your reward in heaven, for in the same way they persecuted the prophets who were before you" (Matthew 5:11-12).*

4. Repaying with Good

In essence, loving our enemies is returning good for evil. I believe that Peter was meditating on Jesus' teaching from Matthew 5 when he wrote 1 Peter 3. Peter was preparing his readers for persecutions, believing that suffering would be the norm for Believers until Jesus' return. Peter wrote,

Do not repay evil for evil or insult with insult, but with blessing, because to this you were called so that you may inherit a blessing. For, "Whoever would love life and see good days must keep his tongue from evil and his lips from deceitful speech. He must turn from evil and do good; he must seek peace and pursue it. For the eyes of the Lord are on the righteous and his ears are attentive to their prayer, but the face of the Lord is against those who do evil." (3:9-12)

I don't know about you, but I want the eyes of the Lord on me and His ears attentive to my prayers! I surely don't want the face of the Lord to be against me. God's loving attention is focused on His people when we use our tongues righteously and when we seek good for others—especially for our enemies.

If people have gossiped about you, make sure that your basic stance is for them. This doesn't mean that you must trust them in the same way you did before. It does mean you should want what is best for them, even at a personal cost. That is how Jesus loved us, isn't it? While we were still His enemies, Christ died for us (Romans 5:8).

Returning blessings for beatings seems crazy to the world, but that's what we do as Believers. Paul's personal testimony was, *"We are fools for Christ.... When we are cursed, we bless; when we are persecuted, we endure it; when we are slandered, we answer kindly" (1Corinthians 4:10, 12-13).* In other words, we bear the family resemblance, living like Christ did. And when we do that, Christ says we will be rewarded.

Great Reward

Jesus asked, *"If you love those who love you, what reward will you get?" (Matthew 5:46).*

Answer: "None."

But the opposite is true, if you love your enemies, you will be richly rewarded. If you love the person who gossips about you, God will pay you back. That is the blessing that Peter said we would inherit (1Peter 3:9). In a paralleled passage Jesus promised, *"Love your enemies, do good to them, and lend to them without expecting to get anything back. Then your reward will be great, and you will be sons of the Most High" (Luke 6:35).*

Date:

I am grateful for:

Dear Father GOD:

Chapter 10
Time to Repent

As much as we may want to, we can't just take words back.

When we are guilty of bearing bad news behind someone's back out of a bad heart, we cannot retrieve the things we have said. The gossip is now out there. Once you hear the sound, you can't take it back."

I see a great deal of shame on the faces of those who have given in to gossip. The choice morsels seemed so irresistible, so tantalizing, at the time of these people's transgression. Now they can't take back what they have said. The damage is done.

Intense Regret
Why do we feel so bad when we have given into gossip?

Gossip Is Sin
Our conscience is warning us that we have offended a holy God who hates gossip. Apostle Paul says in Romans 1, *"The wrath (the hot anger) of God is being revealed from heaven against all the godlessness and wickedness of men who suppress the truth by their wickedness: "They (sinners) are full of envy, murder, strife, deceit and malice. "They are gossips, slanderers, God-haters, insolent, arrogant and boastful; they invent ways of doing evil, they disobey their parents; they are senseless, faithless, heartless, ruthless" (1:29-31). Finally, he says, "Those who do such things deserve death" (1:32).* If we give into the temptation to gossip and have any conscience left, we are going to rightly feel some regret!

Gossip Hurts People
Deep down, we know we are hurting others when we gossip. An old axiom says that gossip hurts at least three people: the one being spoken about, the one hearing the gossip, and the one speaking it. That is true, but the most painful of those positions to be in is the target of the gossip, especially if the story is just a rumor.

Proverbs 12:18 says, *"Reckless words pierce like a sword, but the tongue of the wise brings healing."* When I look back on the time when I have recklessly gossiped about others, one of the things I regret the most is how what I said hurt those people.

Gossip Is Irresistible
On top of offending God and harming others, gossip is something that we can't just take back. The toothpaste is out, and there is no way to stuff it back into

the tube.

Listen to this story:

In a small southern town, a man swept through the community slandering a woman. One day, feeling suddenly remorseful, he begged the woman for forgiveness and offered to undergo penance to make amends. The woman told him to take a feather pillow from his house, cut it open, scatter the feathers to the wind, then return to see her. The man did as he was told, then came to the woman and asked, "Am I now forgiven?"

"Almost," came the response. "You just have to do one more thing. Go and gather all the feathers."

"But that's impossible," the man replied. "The wind has already scattered them."

"Precisely," the woman answered. "And although you truly wish to correct the evil you have done, it is as impossible to repair the damage done by your words as it is to recover the feathers."

So if we can't recover the feathers, what can, and should we do?

1. Repent of Sinful Gossip

The Apostle Paul was just about ready to make his third ministry trip to Corinth, but he was concerned about what he would find when he got there. The Corinthian church had been going steadily downhill:

I am afraid that when I come, I may not find you as I want you to be, and you may not find me as you want me to be. I fear that there may be quarreling, jealousy, outbursts of anger, factions, slander, gossip, arrogance, and disorder. I am afraid that when I come again my God will humble me before you, and I will be grieved over many who have sinned earlier and have not repented of the impurity, sexual sin and debauchery in which they have indulged. (2 Corinthians 12:20-21)

Gossip was a major problem troubling Corinth, and Apostle Paul was concerned that the Corinthians may not have repented of it. Repentance is not just feeling bad about our sin. It is turning away from sin and turning toward the Lord. It is a turn in our heart that changes the directions of our lives. Repentance is also the only way forward after falling prey to sinful gossip.

Confessing Our Sins

The first step of repentance is to confess our sins. To confess means to completely agree with God about our sin. It is telling God that we have sinned by naming what we have done, owning it, and agreeing that it was wrong and an offense against Him. The Bible promises, *"If we confess our sins, (God) is faithful and just and will forgive us our sins and purify us from all unrighteousness" (1 John 1:9)*. What a tremendous promise!

True confession does not fall back on excuses like, "The devil made me do it!" "I didn't want to, but that woman made me gossip." or "Lord, I feel bad about gossiping, but if You knew the circumstances, You'd have done it too."

These are not confessions. A confession says, "Lord, what I did was wrong. I should not have said that. I should not have listened to that. It was against Your law. It hurt someone. It deserves death. I was not glorifying You when I gossiped. I am sorry."

True confessions certainly include our emotions. We should feel bad about having been bad. But confessions also include agreeing with our whole heart that our gossiping was sin.

2. Retract the Sinful Gossip

You never know what people are going to say after a worship service. Like many pastors, I stand at the back door of the church shaking hands with people and greeting them as they leave. Some people like to talk about the sermon, while others chat about the weather or what is going on with their families. Sometimes they ask for prayer.

A few years ago, a young man met me at the door after church and said, "Pastor, I need to ask for your forgiveness. I've been gossiping about you." That took me back a few steps! At first, I didn't know what to say. I really appreciated his sincerity. Finally, I said, "Of course, I forgive you."

"I want you to know that I am not only apologizing to you," the man continued, "I am going to go back to the people I have gossiped to and seek their forgiveness for poisoning their minds against you." And he did. That took some guts, and it was a true sign of repentance.

Seek Godly Counsel

Retracting gossip also takes wisdom and discernment. It is something for us to pray about and to ask the Holy Spirit's guidance on. At times we may need to seek out wise and godly counsel before running around apologizing to people.

There are times when retraction doesn't matter much at all. If we have been gossiping about a celebrity whose face is on the cover of today's True magazine, I don't think it's necessary to send her a letter of apology.

Most of the time our apologies should reach as broadly as those who were affected by our gossip, but in some cases, it might make a relationship worse if you approach people and apologize for gossiping about them. For example, if you gossiped about one of your friend's choices to someone else, it might be best to just apologize to the person with whom you shared it, not to the one about whom you talked. If your friend did not know you thought something bad about her in the first place, it might not help to tell her now. In many ways whether or not we go to every single person involved and apologize depends on the seriousness of what we did. Ask yourself the following:

- How serious was the content of my gossip?
- How seriously could the gossip affect my relationship with this person or impact his or her reputation?
- How far did the bad news travel?

After prayer and godly counsel, if you are not sure whether or not you should confess, I would advise you to err on the side of Jesus' Golden Rule. If your places were switched, would you want that person to come to you and retract the gossip?

From the Heart

The most important confession is to God. If we yawn and say, "Oh, that's not so hard! What is really hard is going to the person I was talking about," then we do not realize how devastatingly wicked our sin really is.

When King David finally repented of his sin with Bathsheba, he wrote a prayer song to the Lord that said, *"Against you, you only, have I sinned and done what is evil in your sight" (Psalm 51:4)*. David did not mean that he had not sinned against Bathsheba, Uriah, and all of Israel. He meant that all sin is first and foremost an offense against a holy God. The wrath of God is being revealed against those who gossip, so we must confess our sin to Him first.

Genuine repentance means confessing more than the words that we used to gossip, but also confessing the heart behind it. Remember, all talk is heart talk. Say, "Lord, I am sorry that I said those things about her. I was being ruled by a lust for power." Or "Lord, my heart was full of hateful grumbling." Or "Lord, I was afraid of the crowd and was not fearing You. Please forgive me." The most amazing thing is that He does.

3. Receive Yeshua's Cleansing

We do not have to lie in self-loathing, condemnation, and regret. We can live as forgiven, cleansed, and pure people. Our scripture says, *"If we confess our sins, he is faithful and just and will forgive us our sins and purify us from all unrighteousness" (1 John 1:9)*.

Are you secretly worried that God will not really forgive you for your gossip (or for any of your sins, for that matter)? Are you afraid that maybe He will bring up your sin again and thrust it in your face? He won't. He is faithful to forgive us if we confess our sins, and He always keeps His promises.

But even more God is faithful to His promises, it would be unjust of God not to forgive. Sure, it seems as if it should be just for God to punish. According to

Scripture, it would! Romans 1:32 says, *"Those who do such things (as gossip) deserve death (by God's righteous decree)."* The just punishment for our sins is God's holy wrath, punishment and condemnation. Yet John says that God is *"faithful and just"* to forgive.

If we confess our sins, he is faithful and just and will forgive us our sins and purify us from all unrighteousness. (1 John 1:9).

Why is forgiving our sins considered just?

Because of the cross. The cross is what makes it just for God to forgive us. Because our sins have already been paid for, it would be unjust for God to refuse forgiveness. John goes on to say,

My dear children, I write this to you so that you will not sin. But if anybody does sin, we have one who speaks to the Father in our defense- Jesus Christ, the Righteous One. He is the atoning sacrifice, for our sins, and not only for ours but also for the sins of the whole world. (1 John 2:1-2)

Jesus Christ died for our sins. He bore the punishment that we deserved for gossiping. He became the atoning sacrifice, or propitiation for our sins, satisfying the wrath of God in our place. Jesus has now become our advocate.

This is why penance is not necessary. Penance, as it is popularly practiced, is taking on a penalty or a punishment to help atone for a sin. But our sin has already been paid for. When He was on the cross, Jesus announced, *"It is finished" (John 19:30).* And it is.

Only because of what Jesus did for us on the cross. God is "faithful and just and will forgive us our sins and purify us from all unrighteousness." Not because of any sincerity of ours, or not because of our righteousness but because of His.

Complete Turnaround

In my research on the subject of gossip, I read quite a few Jewish moral teachings against gossip. Much of what the Jews have said over the years has been very helpful, and we can learn from their reflections on the subject. But most of them do not believe in Jesus as the Messiah, so these Jews have a faulty understanding of grace and no understanding of the cross. They have to make up other things to substitute for it.

One of my favorite Rabbi's teaches that after we stop gossiping, regret what we've done and confess our sins to God, there is still one thing left to do. He says, "Once you have completed these steps, God accepts your return, but it's still on the books, so to speak. Yes, it is noted that it was taken care of, but it's still there." Did you catch that? They go on.

How do you completely edit it out? By going to the next step, called teshuvah gamurah, or "complete return." …. This occurs after you have gone through the steps, time has passed, and God, sometimes with a very good sense of humor, puts you in the same position as when you originally made the mistake, and you do not repeat the mistake. When this occurs, not only are you forgiven, but it's as if you never made the original mistake. It is edited out of the story of your life, as if it had never happened.

We are forgiven and cleansed because we eventually get it right and stop messing up. Believers are forgiven and cleansed only because of the death and resurrection of Jesus Christ.

This righteousness from God comes through faith in Jesus Christ to all who believe. There is no difference, for all have sinned and fall short of the glory of God and are justified freely by His grace through the redemption that came by Christ Jesus. God presented Him as a sacrifice of atonement through faith in his blood. (Romans 3:22-25)

Romans Chapter 1 tells us that we were found guilty, but Romans Chapter 3 declares us not guilty because of the righteousness of Christ reckoned to our account.

No Feather-gathering

We are also not forgiven and cleansed because we ran around town finding each and every one of those feathers that we scattered! We need to be reminded that our words have consequences that we cannot control. But our forgiveness is not tied to finding all the feathers and returning them to the pillowcase. Our forgiveness is tied to the precious blood of Jesus Christ, the atoning sacrifice for our sins.

Receive that cleansing.

Receive it for the first time or for the millionth. If you have never trusted Jesus Christ as your Savior, I invite you to do it now. Yes, your gossiping deserves death, but Jesus died so you would not have to die eternally. Repent right now and trust Jesus Christ as your Savior and Lord, and God will forgive you and purify you from all unrighteousness. He promises! You can be clean.

If you are already a follower of Jesus Christ and have messed up this week by giving in to gossip or some other sin worthy of death, do not wallow in self-hate. Turn to the Lord again for cleansing now. His blood is so powerful!

Repentance is much more powerful than regret. The gospel is much more powerful than gossip. We have seen how the gospel gives us power to resist the gossip, but it also has the power to release forgiveness for us.

Hear this, Believers. God knows where every single feather is and has the sovereign power to find each one and bring them home again. The Bible says that God will work everything to His glory and for His people's good (Rom. 8:28). This is how good the good news is. Receive Yeshua's cleansing and walk in it.

A List of Spiritual Blessings:

How I have seen the Hand of GOD today:

Becoming A Vessel God Can Use

ACCEPT the way God made you

Be **EMPTIED** of self to make room for God.

Allow God to **CLEANSE** you even if the process is painful.

Be **FILLED** and constantly refilled with the Living Water of the Holy Spirit.

POUR OUT your life in ministry as God directs.

Devotion Scriptures

"But we have this treasure in jars of clay to show that this all-surpassing power is from God and not from us." 2 Corinthians 4:7

"Holy, holy, holy is the Lord God Almighty; the whole earth is full of his glory." Isaiah 6:1-3

God Still Heals

"Jesus Christ, the same yesterday, and today, and forever." Hebrews 13:8

I'm alive today to testify that God still heals.

I know you feel like giving up, the road ahead may seem so rough, but don't let go of your faith, stand on His word. God has the final say.

"He sent His Word and healed them and delivered them from their destruction."
Psalm 107:20

By the Word of My Mouth, I speak over you!
Blessings of Health
Blessings of Wealth
The BLESSING is on you!

Moving Forward

Philippians 3:14
"I press toward the mark for the prize of the high calling of God in Christ Jesus."
I'm not going back,
I'm moving ahead!

Oh Lord, I will serve you every day, all my life I will praise you. Hear me calling now I pray; I will worship you only.
Now I bow before your throne Lord, Holy Father, hear me calling. This is your Servant's Prayer, Lord. Amen

"Then shalt thou call, and the Lord shall answer, thou shalt cry, and He shall say, here I am."
Isaiah 58:9

Breaking of the Dawn

You may be broken
Tears may be falling all through the night
But God has not forsaken, He's gonna lead you into the light

"Weeping may endure for a night, but joy is coming in the morning light."
Psalm 30:5

"So, if the Son sets you free, you are free indeed."
John 8:36

Fortifications for the Mind, Body, and Spirit

Father God,
We are precious jewels to you, help us remember and the good that people do, as you Lord do to us, Hallelujah!

Father God,
Thank you for peace in the midnight hour and your guidance in my rest as I dwell in your majesty, Hallelujah!

Father God,
It's a new day for favor; please release your Ruach breath, so I can help change the world one soul at a time, Hallelujah!

Father God,
I desire more of you, as I carry the cross, please keep me in your narrow way each and every day, Amen!

My God,
I sit in awe of your majesty because you allow me to be close enough to hear your breath, Hallelujah!

Father,
This is the Year of the Lord, and your great manifestation, send me I'll go, Hallelujah!

What is the **Prayer of Submission**?

Defined as:

Being submissive tells God that He cannot only trust but use you. Submission is an act of obedience. We often tell the Lord that we will follow Him. That we will go where He tells us to go, do what He tells us to do, and we ask Him to use us in the way that He sees fit.

My Thoughts:

What is the **Prayer of Petition**?

Defined as:

A request made for something desired, especially a respectful or humble request, as to a superior or to one of those in authority; a supplication or prayer: a petition for aid; a petition to God for courage and strength.

My Thoughts:

What is the **Prayer of Agreement**?

Defined as:

The prayer of agreement usually involves two or more people coming together and deciding to pray concerning anything in particular that they desire.

My Thoughts:

What is the **Prayer of Release**?

Defined as:
A prayer for when you need to release in order to know peace.
Sometimes we need to stand and fight, but we need to release as well.

My Thoughts:

What is the **Prayer of Spir**

Defined as:
If you seek to pray in the Holy Spirit, you seek to develop the love character of Jesus Christ, and seek to conform your prayers to desires that are not lustful, but rather, desires that develop your capacity for love.

My Thoughts:

What is the **Prayer of Intercession**?

Defined as:
The act of interceding, prayer, petition, or entreaty in favor of another.

My Thoughts:

What is the **Prayer of Binding and**

Defined as:
To bind and to loose simply means to forbid by an indisputable authority and to permit by an indisputable authority.

My Thoughts:

What is the **Prayer of Healing**?

Defined as:

Faith healing is the practice of prayer and gestures (such as laying on of hands) that are believed by some to elicit divine intervention in spiritual and physical healing.

My Thoughts:

Ruling Your World

4   Now Deborah, a prophet, the wife of Lappidoth, was leading[a] Israel at that time. 5 She held court under the Palm of Deborah between Ramah and Bethel in the hill country of Ephraim, and the Israelites went up to her to have their disputes decided. 6 She sent for Barak son of Abinoam from Kedesh in Naphtali and said to him, "The Lord, the God of Israel, commands you: 'Go, take with you ten thousand men of Naphtali and Zebulun and lead them up to Mount Tabor. 7 I will lead Sisera, the commander of Jabin's army, with his chariots and his troops to the Kishon River and give him into your hands.'"

8   Barak said to her, "If you go with me, I will go; but if you don't go with me, I won't go."

9   "Certainly, I will go with you," said Deborah. "But because of the course you are taking, the honor will not be yours, for the Lord will deliver Sisera into the hands of a woman." So, Deborah went with Barak to Kedesh. 10 There Barak summoned Zebulun and Naphtali, and ten thousand men went up under his command. Deborah also went up with him. (Judges 4:4-10)

As Deborah ruled her world, may you also know the gift of authentic love. Stop waiting for the approval and applause of others, they will never celebrate your growth, healing or empowerment.

On your growing list of things to do, protect and increase your time for you. Our wholeness is important. Stop being a part of bad habits, making poor decisions that don't lead to an abundant life.

"See Yourself the Way God Sees You"

Heavenly Father, thank you for your love, this day like no other day. Thank you for waking me up and giving me the breath of life.

Thank you for your loving grace that abounds in my life. I commit myself to your hands, sustain me and favor me on this day. Please never leave my side. Carry me in your protective hands, let everything that I do bring glory to you. Amen!

Reflecting and Journaling

1. Pulling together everything you have learned throughout this study, what are the key truths for you to keep in mind for becoming a Psalm 15 man or woman? Or a Proverbs 31 woman?

    _____
    _____
    _____
    _____
    _____
    _____
    _____

2. The devil wants you to live in defeat, and he says to us, "You can't be completely forgiven, just like you can't gather up all those feathers."
    How do you respond to this statement?

    _____
    _____
    _____
    _____
    _____
    _____
    _____

3. How is the gospel of Jesus Christ greater than gossip? How can you hold your head up and walk in renewed victory?

    _____
    _____
    _____
    _____
    _____

4. Have you ever gone to one of your victims and asked for forgiveness from him or her? Why or why not? How did it go?

    _____
    _____
    _____
    _____
    _____
    _____

5. What does it mean to you to forgive or be forgiven?

_____

_____

_____

_____

_____

_____

6. Can you still enter into the Kingdom of Heaven holding an offense?

_____

_____

_____

_____

_____

_____

7. What effect does believing in the Kingdom of Heaven have on your life when you find yourself gossiping?

_____

_____

_____

_____

_____

8. How does gossip affect your integrity?

_____

_____

_____

_____

9. What excuses have you used to try to justify your gossip?

_____

_____

_____

_____

_____

10. When was the last time you prayed against gossip?

_____

_____

_____

_____

11. What and when have you taught anyone you know about gossip?

_____
_____
_____
_____
_____
_____

12. How are you treating people's reputation with care, both male and female?

_____
_____
_____
_____
_____
_____

13. Read 3 John 9-10. Is there someone you know that needs to be called out for malicious gossip?

_____
_____
_____
_____
_____

How can you encourage your family to see God's blessing in their lives?

_____
_____
_____
_____
_____
_____

14. How can you lead your family, friends, and community deeper into the deeper relationship with God?

_____
_____
_____
_____

15. How can you encourage loving small talk?

_____

_____

_____

_____

_____

16. Read Colossians 3:12-17 and Galatians 5:13-15 and contrast the passages. Does your family have a commitment to build fellowship with others within the community?

_____

_____

_____

_____

    Is the commitment formal or informal?

_____

_____

_____

_____

    If informal, do you need to formalize it?

_____

_____

_____

_____

17. What does it mean to be an immature believer?

_____

_____

_____

_____

18. Growing closer to the Lord should be the most important thing in your life. Why?

_____

_____

_____

_____

19. What are the five (5) signs of a mature believer?

_____

_____

_____

_____

20. Mature believers grow less dependent on themselves and increasingly dependent on Yeshua (Jesus). True or False? _____

Does this apply to you?

_____

_____

_____

_____

Declare and Decree

Declaration Steps

1. I declare and decree that I am closer to God than ever before.

2. I declare and decree that I have divine intelligence already inside of me with clarity, sharpness, and precision on a whole new level.

3. I declare and decree that I am abundantly blessed in wisdom and revelation knowledge.

4. I declare and decree that I am walking in a dimension of God's dunamis power and authority. His signs, wonders, and miracles are a gift and His promise to all who believe.

5. I declare and decree that I am a living vessel full of Holy Ghost power and miraculous breakthroughs.

6. *But you are a chosen people, a royal priesthood, a holy nation, God's special possession, that you may declare the praises of Him who called you out of darkness into His wonderful light. (1 Peter 2:9).*

Recognizing gossip for myself:

Dear Father GOD:

Date:

Am I walking in immaturity?

How I have seen the Hand of GOD today:

I am so grateful for a renewed mind and maturity:

Dear Father GOD:

Date:

Transforming the Mindset

Let's look at the lyrics to all these songs. Where do you see yourself in this historical journey? This book is focusing on gossiping, being immature, and purposing to hurt others by the words that come out of our mouth and heart.

All these songs talk about the Glory of God:

Star- Spangled Banner (1814)
America (My Country, 'Tis of Thee) (1831)
America The Beautiful (1895)
Lift Every Voice and Sing (1900)
Put your Hand in the Hand (1970 - Anne Murray)

Then here we have Dr. Martin Luther King Jr. writing a speech called, "I Have a Dream!" (1963)

Dr. King spoke many vital, pivotal points in his speech. He cried out to the Lord and all nations to remind us that his own children would one day not be judged by the color of their skin, but by the content of their character. So let us not wallow in the valley of despair even though we still face much turmoil and dangers of this world and society.

Dr. King still had a dream that one day, not just in the state of Alabama, that little black boys and little black girls would be able to join hands with little white boys and little white girls as sisters and brothers. That each of us would respect, honor, and love one another on purpose. Let's think about this while we spend so much energy, time, and space, gossiping, backbiting, and slandering each other with our words straight from the heart, and wonder why sickness and disease is at an all-time high. Dr. King truly believed as do I, that we would be able to work together, pray, laugh, dance, read, struggle, and stand strong together, knowing that one day we would all be free. He spoke these words sayin he had been to the mountaintop like Moses in the Bible. And seen the promise land where a society of black people would have peace and equ rights. He knew that he may not get there with us, just as Moses did no go to the promise land, but Moses anointed Joshua to take his place. How many of us have others standing in the gap for us, praying for us, and believing that all of us are truly created equal. But Dr. Martin Luth King Jr. never stopped believing in hope, love, peace, and his dream. Gc has promised us that He will never leave us nor forsake us. So, I will leav you with this, "Be the Change that You want to see and Be the Change that You need to Be!" The world will, become a better place when you make the choice to be a better YOU! And if God be for you who can b against us. Amen!

The best thing we
can do is be
a servant of God.

It does good to
stand up and serve
others.

Love One Another

Dancing to the Glory of the Lord

I'm free

Images taken at White Sands, New Mexico

They
WHISPERED
TO HER
YOU
CANNOT
WITHSTAND
THE STORM
She
WHISPERED BACK
I am
THE STORM

T. MILLS

To connect with Dr. Mavis E. Morisseau for speaking, teaching, life coaching, and ministry engagements, please visit the following website: twpkministry.com or scan the QR code.

SCAN ME

About the Illustrator

Ms. Tonya Mills has worked in education for over 25 years and loves to be creative with digital art and illustrations. Her book designs include, 'Created by God, so we must be special" by Dr. Mavis Morisseau. Tonya has a gift and passion for designing book covers, custom logos, posters, and 3D Designs.

Image citations:

Picture descriptions from Pixaby.com. Free for commercial use. No attribution required.

- Dead Sea, Israel
- Jerusalem Israel Old Town Walls The Rock
- Basilica Of The Holy Sepulchre
- Israel Negev Timna Park Rocks Acacia Tree Dry
- Tree Lonely Rocks Stones Rocky Grounds
- Sunset Sea Water Sky Coast Israel North
- Beach Landscape Hawaii
- Martin Luther King Civil Rights Activist
- Hands Team United Together People Unity Teamwork

Blue flowers on Journal Pages from Pixaby.com. Free for commercial use. No attribution required.

- Decor Decoration Jewelry Flower Blue Silver

Collage images taken by Author at White Sands,

New Mexico 'They Whispered to you' image

attributed to Akosua Hadassah Other images are

original artwork by the Illustrator

www.ingramcontent.com/pod-product-compliance
Lightning Source LLC
Chambersburg PA
CBHW051539120626
46551CB00013B/1289